They Call Me
"The Ghost Guy"

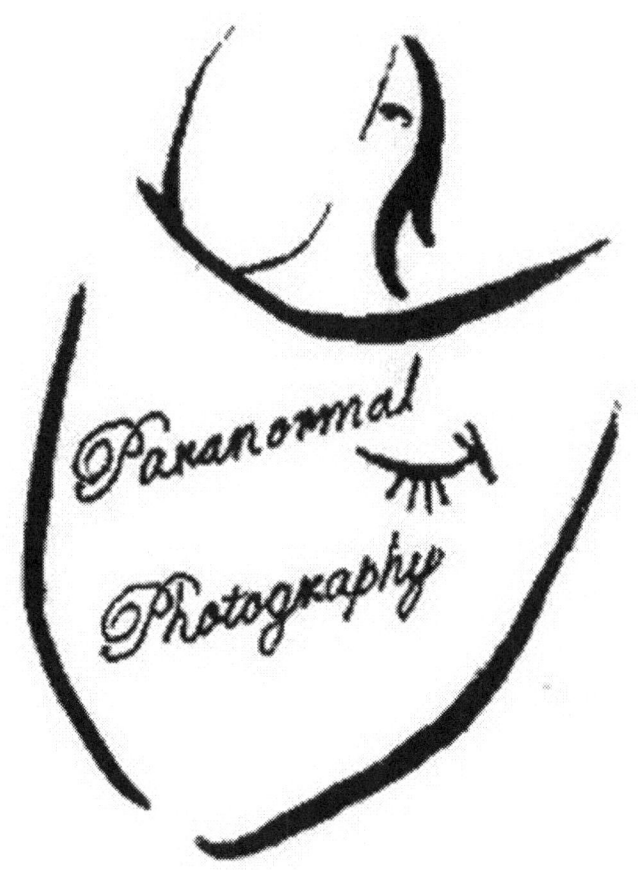

They Call Me "The Ghost Guy"

www.paranormalphotography.com

Published by LuLu
www.LuLu.com

ISBN: 978-1-4303-1261-1

Acknowledgement

A special heartfelt thanks for their helpful suggestions, editing and support to the family and friends that helped us bring this book to life: Alice and Chuck Stump, Joel Lewis, John and Judy Whitaker, Michael "Deerfeather" Gilszmer, Steve Harrison, Blake Crouch, Tom Dongo, Brad Steiger, and Andrea Busick.

Dedicated to our children:

Joel Lewis

Adam Richard

Danielle Richard

Forward

By Blake Crouch

I first encountered Michael "The Ghost Guy" Richard on a cool, Halloween night at The Arts Center in Durango, Colorado. In the spirit of the holiday, Mike was presenting a slideshow of something he called "Paranormal Photography." As a suspense novelist, I was immediately intrigued. Over the course of the next forty-five minutes, the crowd was wowed with some of the most awe-inspiring spirit-world images we'd ever seen, accompanied by strange, (often funny, sometimes sinister) stories of how those images were captured. Many of those photographs and stories are contained in the pages to come.

A few years later, while doing research for a novel, I gave Mike a call and asked if I could come along on one of his photo-shoots. He generously agreed, and I found myself strolling through the halls of the Jarvis Suites, a haunted hotel in downtown Durango.

We went down into the dusty basement and looked at an old drawing on the concrete walls that no one knew how it got there. We walked down quiet corridors, into empty rooms, and I would watch Mike get a feel for the space. Often, he'd just shake his head and walk out, but occasionally, he'd get the sense that the room was "heavy" with some energy or presence, and would begin to take pictures.

The wonderful thing about this book is that it gives us a rare window into one of the most mysterious professions you'll ever read about. As I learned on my tag-along with Mike, paranormal photography isn't just about snapping pictures of spirits stuck between worlds. It's about learning to pay attention to things we might ordinarily overlook. It's art, it's history, even service, inasmuch as Mike is often there to help a spirit move on who for some reason can't.

From abandoned ghost towns to Anasazi ruins to the haunted halls of corporate America, the bizarre, utterly fascinating journey of Michael Richard is like nothing you've read before. When finished with this book, you may very well give more credence to the eerie noise your house makes in the early morning hours.

Blake Crouch
Durango, Colorado
April 2007

Content

They Call Me
"The Ghost Guy"

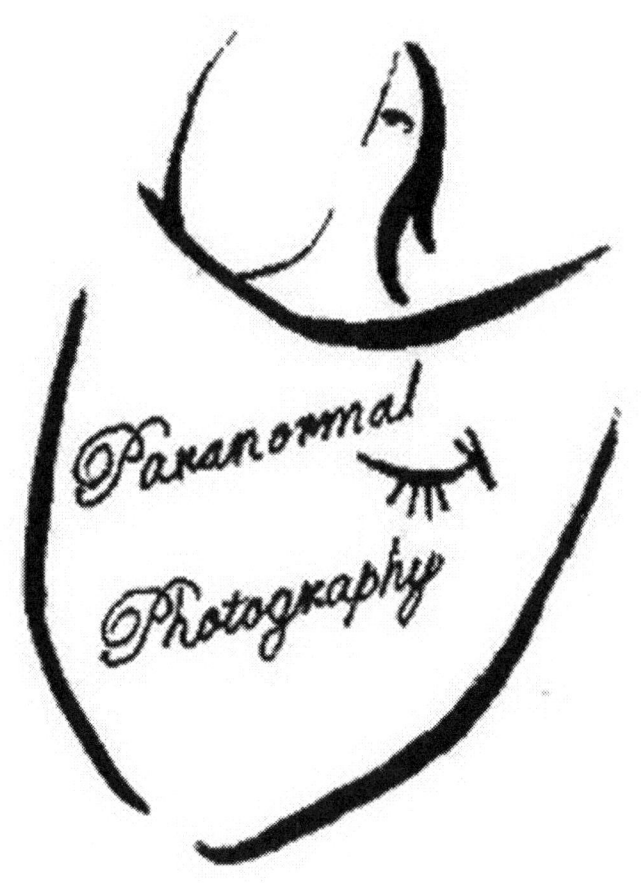

Introduction

First let me introduce myself, I am Michael Richard. Today I am known nationally as "The Ghost Guy." I grew up in a world where the paranormal was taboo and not to be spoken about. If you saw, heard or just felt the spirit world you were considered crazy or just plain weird. Now, looking back, I can see that the paranormal world has had a positive change on my life.

People often ask me if I ever get frightened. The answer is yes! Dealing with the paranormal world on a regular basis can be extremely difficult. It is sometimes hard to stay focused on what you are doing when everything around you is chaotic. I've seen a lot of different and strange things. But by working with respect for the entities, some spirits will pose or even invite me to take their pictures. Because of this, we have rarely encountered hostile spirits or been attacked.

Most cases I investigate without other people present. I pick up on more when no one else is talking or making a lot noise. Plus, most spirits do not like a lot of activity in this world, it frightens or just annoys them. Sometimes, I do take my wife with me when I shoot, it helps to have a second opinion. Plus, she knows the paranormal world and the routine I use. I do not use unnecessary equipment during shoots that can interfere with the spirits' energy. Other than a camera, most of the equipment used these days by paranormal investigators is just to impress the living. If you rely on meters to tell you when an entity is present, that entity will be gone before a camera can be brought up and focused.

We all seek the world of the paranormal. It's amazing how many people go through life looking for signs from the other side and don't recognize them. When in actuality, the signs are there everyday. All we have to do is pay attention to our surroundings.

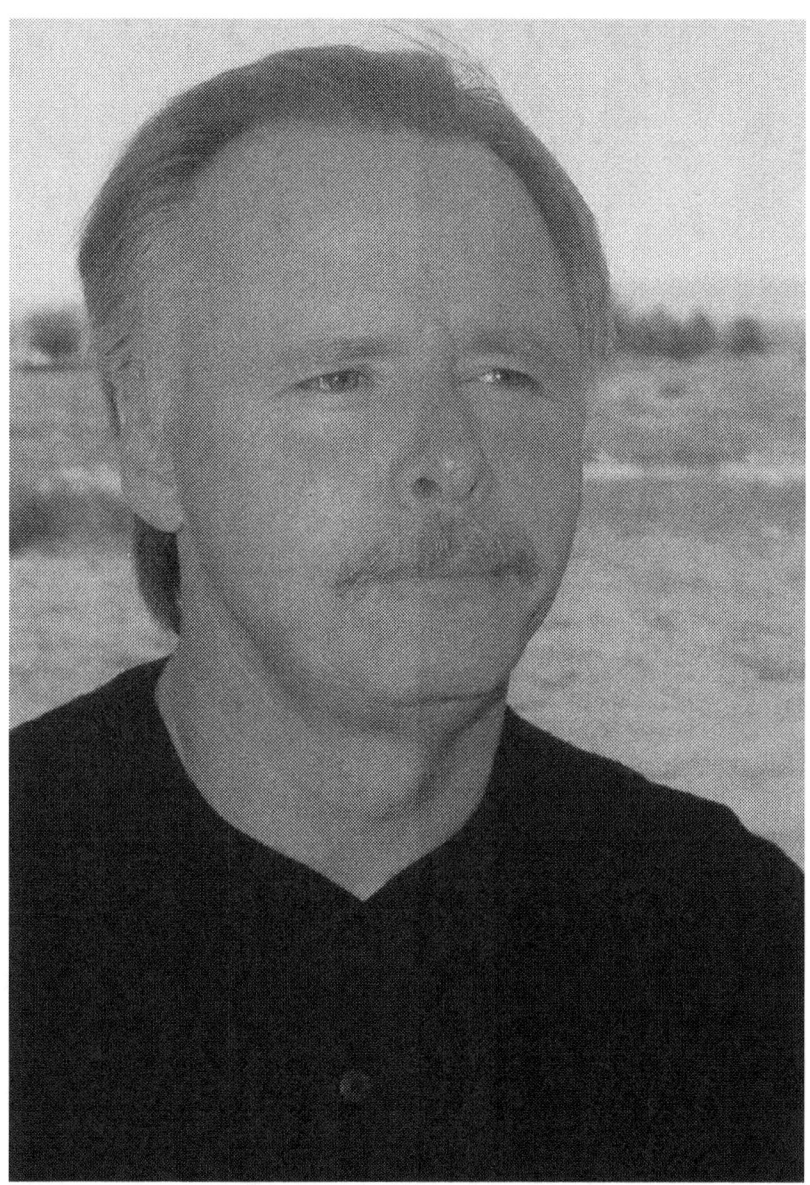

Michael Richard - Photo taken by Susan Richard

My Introduction to the Paranormal

For Mother's Day weekend in 1966, my parents decided to take a three day weekend and drive down to Long Beach, CA. At the time we were living in San Fernando Valley and they thought that this would be a good break without going too far away with the five youngest kids and my aunt (The three oldest kids were back east visiting family and my youngest brother was yet to be born.).

We stayed in a hotel on the beach. The first morning, we all went down to eat breakfast at a restaurant close by. We finally hit the beach late that morning. Around 1 pm, my parents took three of us kids with them and walked along the shallows in the surf. As we were walking along, I stepped off of the land shelf and dropped another 6 ft into the ocean. As I fell, I gasped and took in a lot of water. I can remember sinking to the bottom and then a huge white light engulfed me. The light felt alive and female. It gave me a

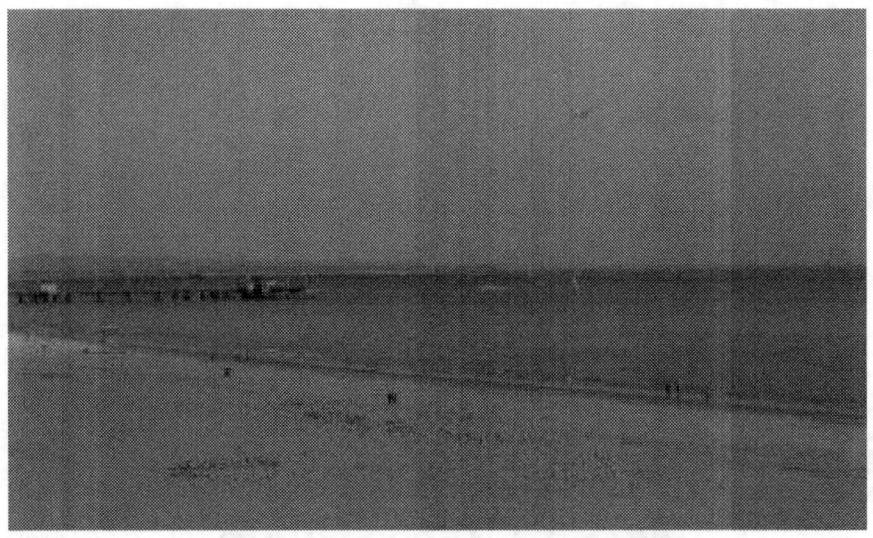

Photograph of Long Beach courtesy of Chuck and Alice Stump.

feeling of comfort and pushed me toward the surface. Just as I was breaking the surface, my father grabbed my arm and dragged me to the beach. He proceeded to hit me on the back until I expelled all the water I had swallowed. My Aunt Sandy kept asking if I was okay. I told her that everything looked funny. She said that was because of all the water I swallowed. But that wasn't it at all.

For the rest of the trip and when we got home, I would look closely at people around me. I could see this colored foggy mist around everyone (years later I could see this mist around everything). My parents repeatedly asked me what I was looking at and I would reply, "Nothing."

About a year later, my parents had a business associate over to the house. When I answered the door, of course I checked out her foggy mist and was fascinated by how white and glowing hers was compared to others I had seen. Immediately she said, "So you can see auras, very good Michael." That is when I found out what had been happening to me this whole time.

Another year passed, and I saw this glowing white amebic figure walking down the sidewalk with an older lady of this world. Within the next week I saw another one. Then a neighbor of ours died in a car accident. Just hours later, I saw another one of these weird amebic figures and saw his persona in it. That's when it dawned on me that these figures are ghosts. Since then I have seen the paranormal. I can see auras and spirits. Sometimes I can even hear or feel the other side.

Ten years later, I become a photographer in the Navy. When I got out I continued with professional photography, but it was several more years before I started photographing the paranormal.

The Beginning of my Paranormal Photography Career

It started as a joke. My brother was working for a large technology based corporation in San Jose California back in 1984. They were having a problem in one of their outer buildings. The security guards kept finding the lights on. When the guards went to turn out the lights, they would also find all the doors unlocked. They proceeded to turn off the lights and lock the doors. When they checked the next hour, they would find all the lights on and the doors unlocked. Inside the building were three security cameras to pick up any activity taking place, the only thing that showed on these cameras were the guards turning out the lights and locking the doors. My brother jokingly asked me to go and take pictures of the perpetrators since I was the professional photographer. My initial thoughts were that a prankster was involved. Boy was I ever wrong!

When I arrived at the site, I was introduced to the head of security, Cynthia, a woman who seemed happy with my arrival. We had sat down and were discussing the situation, when I overheard some of the guards talking. The word "ghost" kept coming up. Now I was intrigued! I made arrangements for later that day to check out the building where the ruckus was going on. My appointment was for 11:00pm.

With plenty of time to check out the area, I found myself in a large mall called Eastridge. It had several book stores I wanted to checkout. When I walked down the photography section in one of the book stores, a book fell off of the shelf in front of me. Picking up the book, I was amazed to read the title, "Photographing the Spirit World." Now things were getting weird! Somebody, or something, was trying to get a point across and it had my full attention. I went straight up to the register to buy the book. When the woman asked where I found the book, I explained to her that it fell off the shelf and I wanted to buy it. She said that she was the owner of the store had never seen the book before. Since the book was not in her inventory, she gave me the book free of charge. After some research, we discovered that the book had been out of print for over 10 years. At this point the whole process ceased to be a joke. Now I don't know about anybody else, but I can take a hint.

That night, I was able to photograph several paranormal activities within that particular building. Later that week, the head of security did some research at a local library. Cynthia used mostly old newspaper articles on microfiche. She found out that over thirty years earlier a couple had crashed their car into a tree and died. This was in the exact spot where the building now stood.

That's when I formed Paranormal Photography and people started to call me "The Ghost Guy."

The photographs on the next two pages are the results of my shoot that night. The first image shows spirit energy directly over the table against the wall. The closest light source in that hallway was over the TV. The second image shows the same area. However, the light had gone out above the TV and the spirit energy had intensified. The last photograph was taken in a completely dark hallway. All the light you see is from spirit energy.

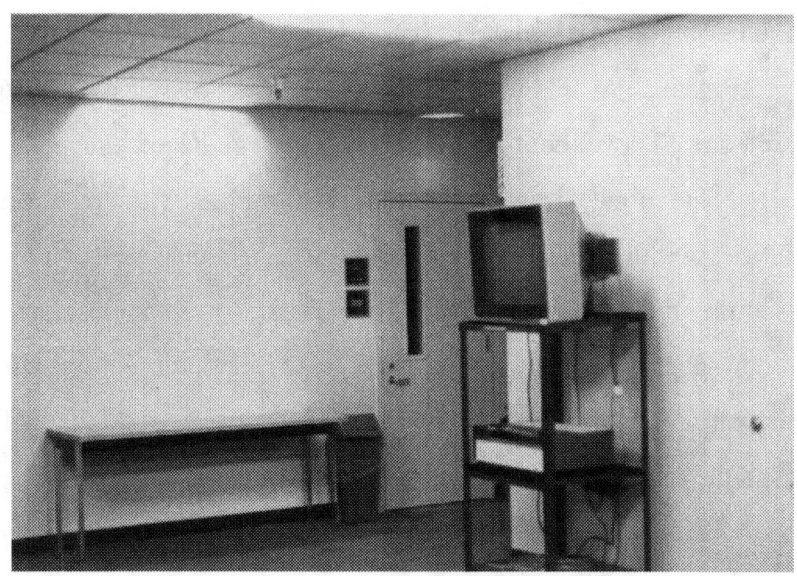

The spirit energy intensifies and shorts out the hall light

between the shots shown above and below.

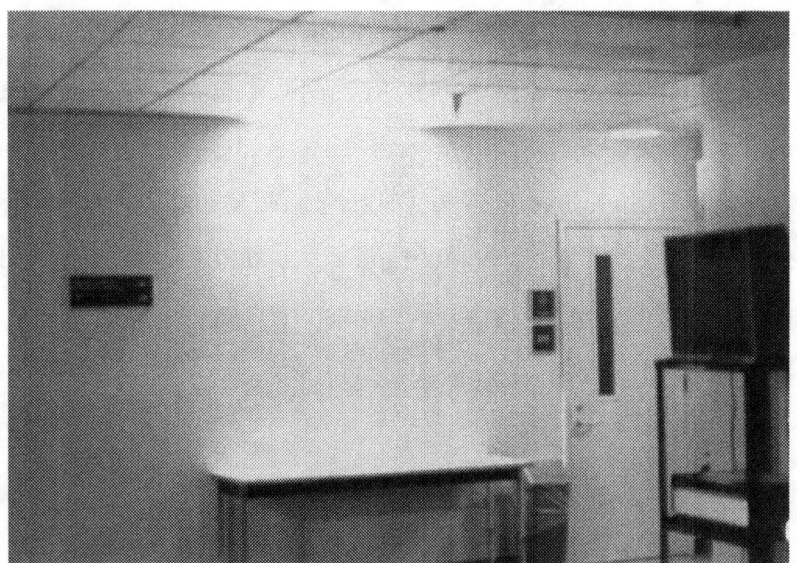

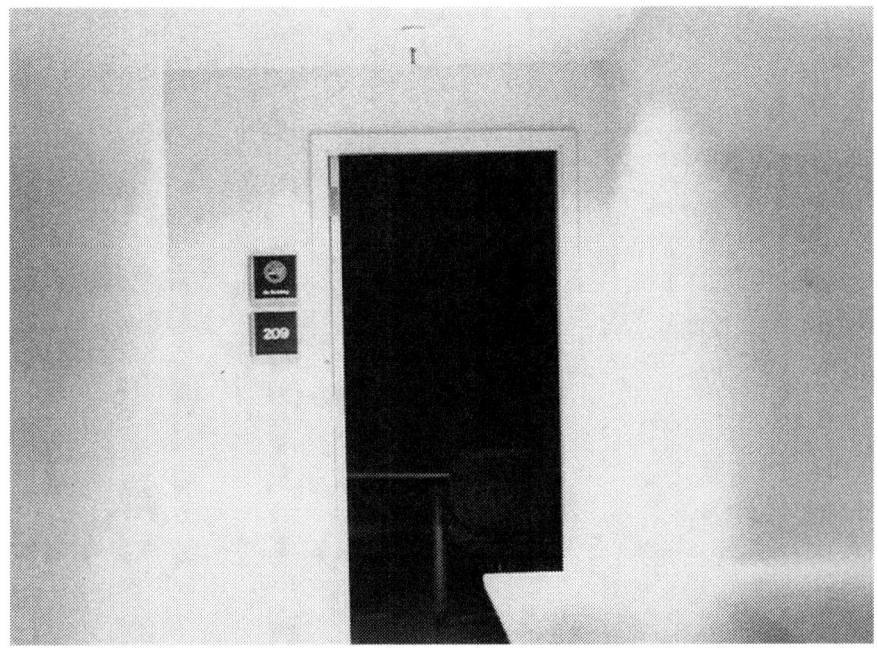

This shot shows only spirit energy, there is no light on in this section of the building.

An Overview of

Paranormal Photography

In the ensuing years, I have developed my technology of taking pictures of ghosts, spirits and other phenomenon. This has been several years of trial and error process. I have used many types and brands of film and several types of cameras. I have found that only two types of film, high speed and infrared, will give me the detail and dependability I demand. You can, however, get interesting results with regular film. I have also found that manual cameras are best. The newer technology incorporated in cameras today interferes with the images we get with high speed and infrared film. The results are suspect.

Spirits and ghosts are generally a shy bunch, although some can be very bold. They do not like crowds or chaos on this side.

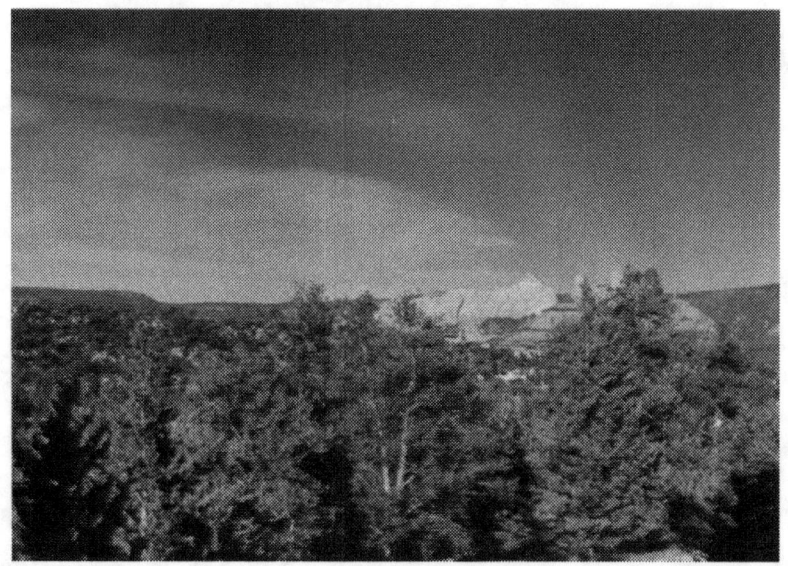

The image above is infrared film and the image below is high speed film.

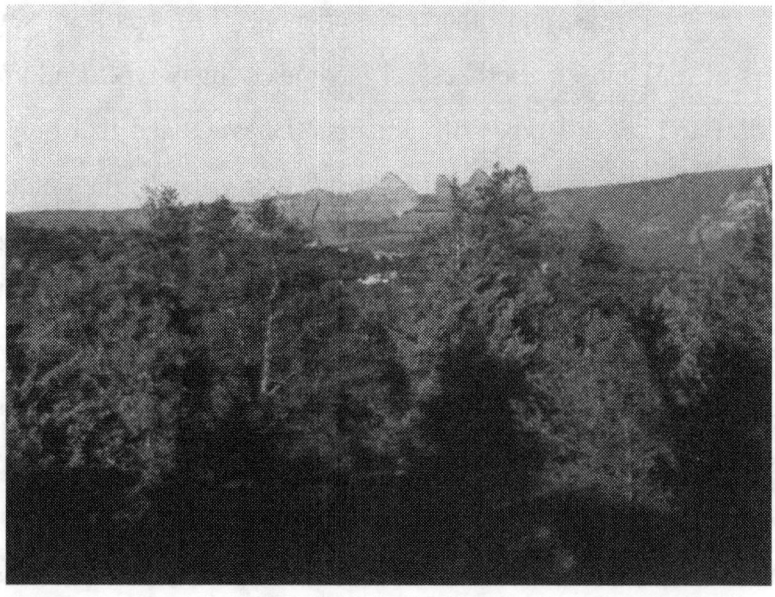

Sightings are generally in quiet areas without a lot going on at the time. This is why I limit the number of people that can be around while I do a shoot. In addition, spirits do have the ability to choose whether they want to show up on film. If a spirit does not want its picture taken, it doesn't matter if the camera is pointed right at them or not. It is possible, however, to get a photograph of them when they are unaware.

There are many types of paranormal phenomenon. In true hauntings there are two types; spirits and ghosts. Spirits are beings that have come over for a particular reason. Either they want to get a message to this side or they are here to give comfort to someone specific. These beings include spirits that lived in this world before and beings who never lived here. Those who have only lived in the paranormal world include such beings as gnomes, fairies, the wee people, etc. Ghosts on the other hand, are lost souls who haven't found their path to move on to the next world.

Other than true hauntings, you might actually have an imprint in time. This type of "haunting" is when the events happen at the same time, place and way every time like the original occurrence. At this point in my career, the only photographs of an imprint that I have gotten are of buildings that are no longer standing. These imprints generally occur only after a thunderstorm.

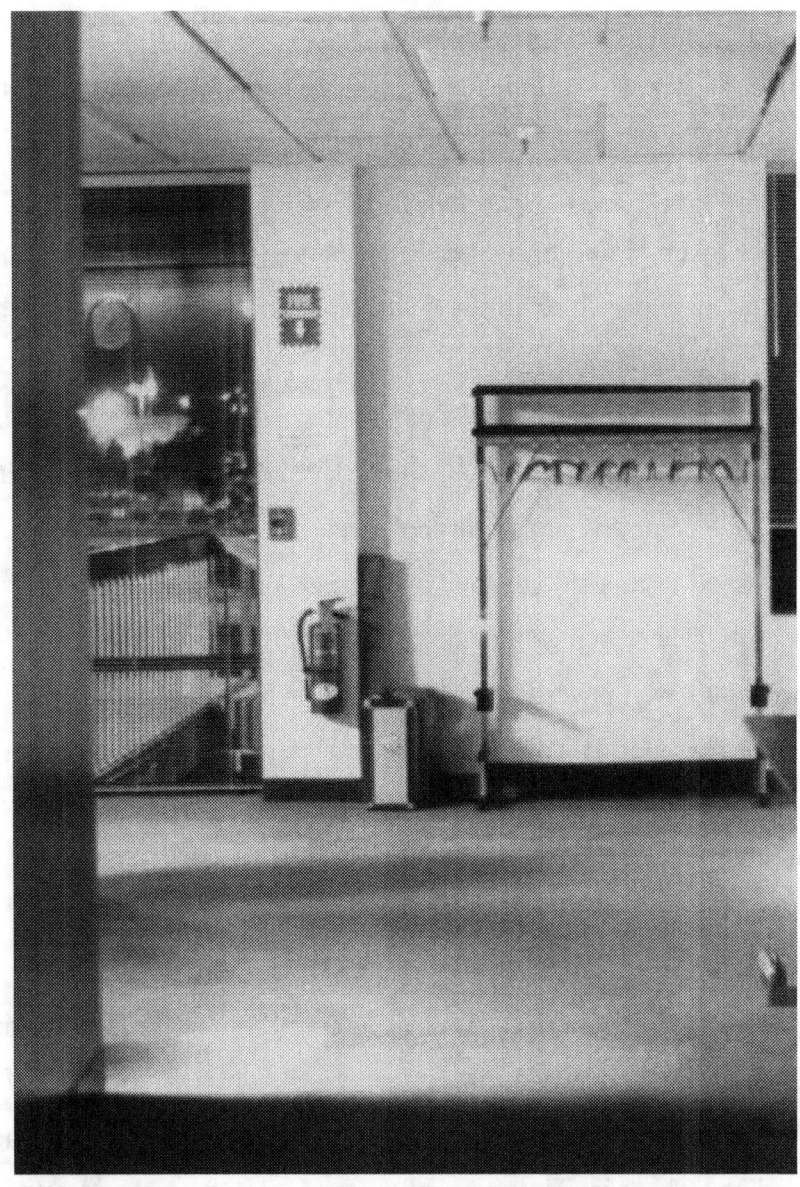

Looking out the window, you can see the image of a factory that existed in the 1930s.

To ensure that my results are accurate, I go through several steps for each shoot.

First, I use the manual cameras that are incapable of taking double exposures.

When I arrive at the site of possible activity, I will determine if I feel any presences. If I do, I start with filling out the following record forms:

On these forms I gather such information as the existence and location of electrical fields, windows, time of day, weather conditions, a description of the activity and the names of the witnesses. The following picture is an example of the forms explaining the shot and determining if the unusual image is paranormal in origin or not.

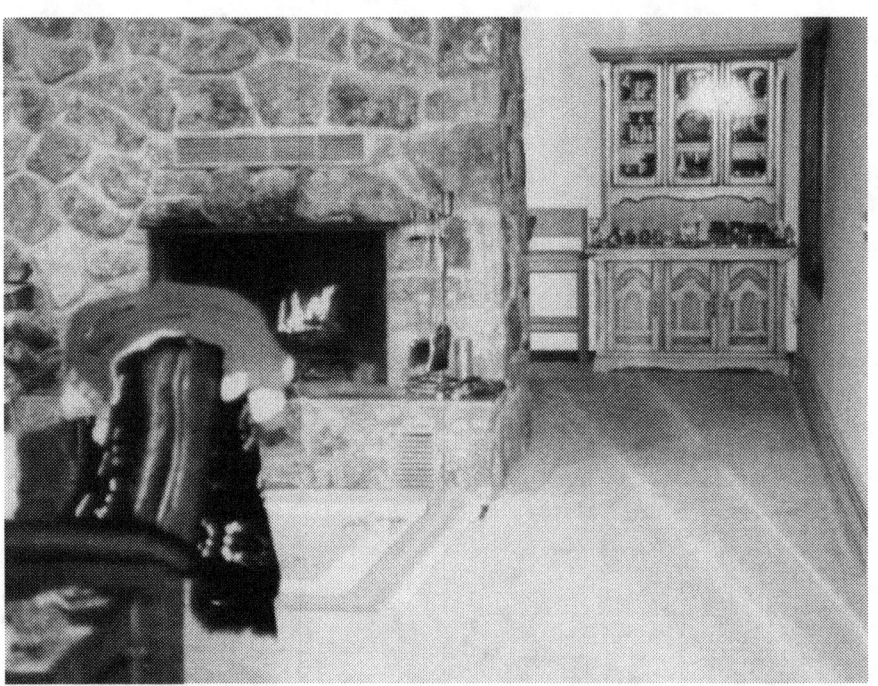

The light seen in the china cabinet in this photograph could have been confused with spirit energy, except the forms told us that this was a reflection of a light fixture.

After filling out the forms, I will set up the time for my shoot and request that everyone leaves for the specified time. Frequently my wife, Susan, will follow me around and take pictures with regular film for our record. Sometimes she will get some activity in her shots.

After my shoot, I will send my film off to an independent lab and Susan will send her film to a different lab. This way there is no question of my tampering with the negatives or the lab being influenced by the different film results. High speed and infrared film need special handling. No light can be allowed to reach the film before it has been processed. We either find labs in the location we are that can handle specialized film, or we will mail it out to a couple of labs that we trust across the country.

Not every shoot is successful. It depends on a number of factors. The spirits must be willing, even if in the end it is a grudging willingness. There needs to be no interference on this side, such as electrical interference or negative energy. The level of energy present, will enhance or be a detriment to the quality and detail of the pictures. That is why some of my best shots come in groups.

Metaphysical Shop

In 1985, a friend had called me to see if I was interested in doing an investigation of a metaphysical shop in northern California. This shop was, to say the least, having some problems. Every night someone or something was removing things from the shelves and placing them in the back storage area. Rarely did this entity actually break anything.

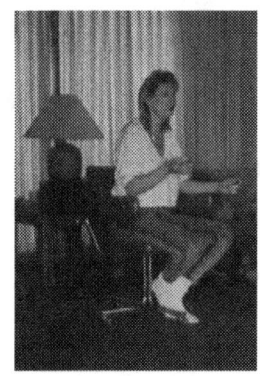

Fredrika

I called the owners of the shop to discuss the problem they were having and what could be done about it. I also called my psychic friend, Fredrika, to talk about what we could do. We decided to meet with the owners the next day to get things started. We arrived early to find one of the shop owners cleaning up a large mess. He was very glad to see us.

We sat down to listen to the details of his story of the nightly movements. I decided to take some test shots of the area to get a feel for what was really happening. The next day I got my pictures back and everything seemed normal on film. The burglar alarm never went off, so it could not have been a corporal person that was causing the disturbances. Since the entity would not come out while anyone was present, the owners and I agreed on setting up cameras that would take pictures during the night when an infrared transmitter beam was broken.

I set up three transmitter beams with three cameras. When I came back the next day to check on my equipment; the cameras had taken four pictures. It was a rough two days before I got the film back. The first picture only showed the shop. The following three images (on pages 28 -29) show the fantastic results I got. The last image is the photograph known as "Spirit Shop."

I sat down with Fredrika to discuss how we could get rid of the angry spirit. She suggested talking to him to find out why he was there. Some psychics think that the spirits can be forced to leave against their will. Fredrika, however, thought that she could talk the spirit into leaving. I found that idea amusing at first then I realized that she was serious.

That night we went back to talk to this spirit with another

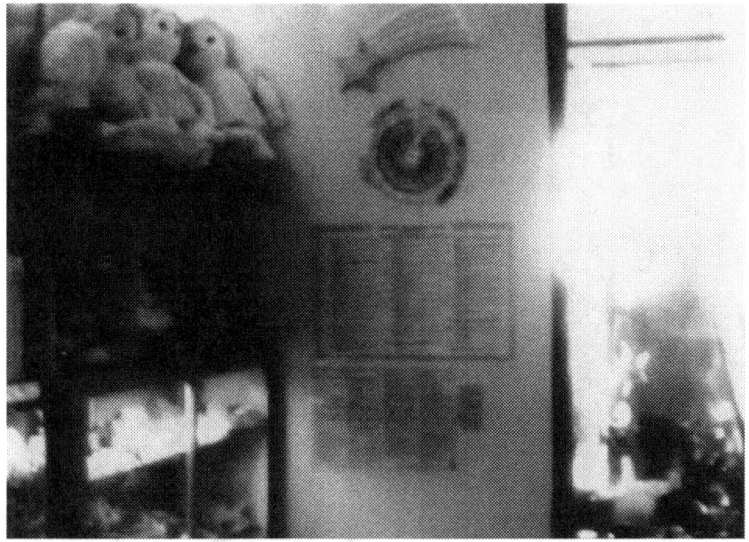

Look close through the spirit energy on the right and you will see a figure.

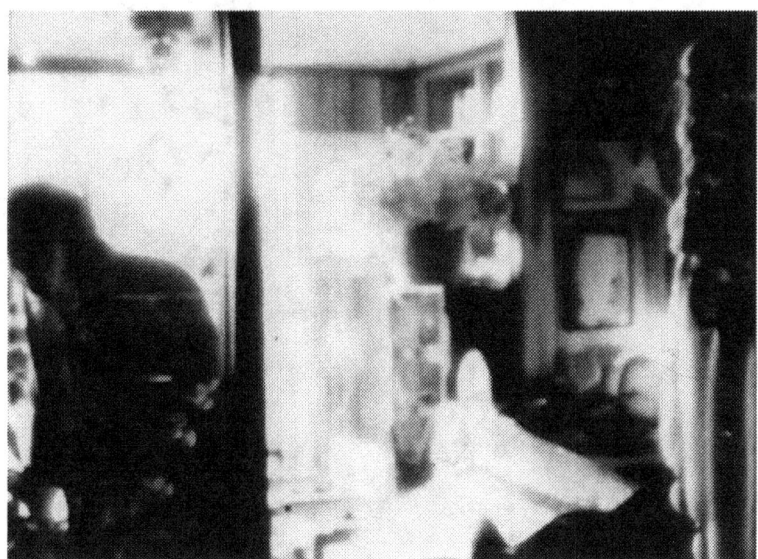

Notice the shelving and other objects visible through the figure and the left.

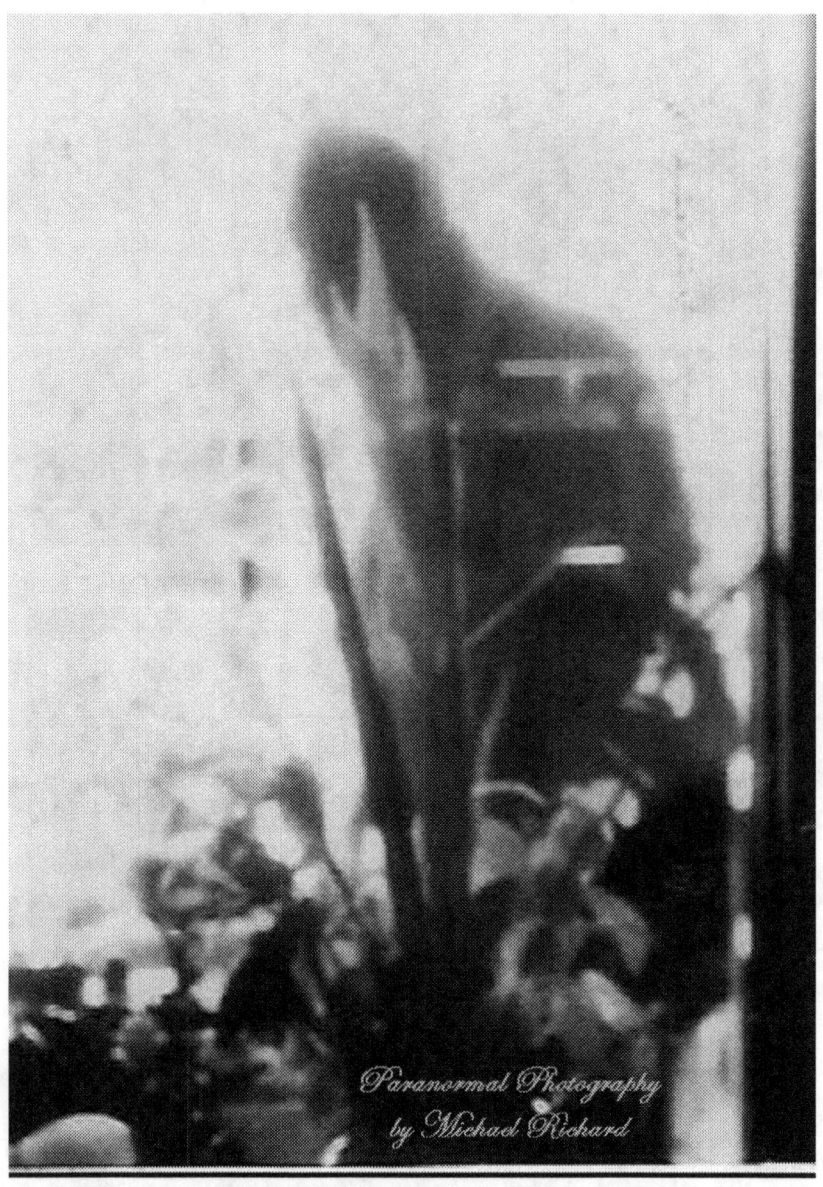

"Spirit Shop" shows a transparent figure with some plants and shelves behind him.

psychic, Carol Fox, to see if we could solve his problem. When we arrived you could feel the anger in the air. At that point I was willing to leave, but Fredrika was adamant about getting him to move on.

Talking to him, Fredrika found out that he was killed in a car accident before the building went up.   It had turned out that this man was a christian and thought he was doing some good by destroying the shop. Fredrika explained to him that everybody is loved by the creator no matter what their beliefs and that it was time for him to move on. With this information, he agreed and left.

A Call for Help

Another small town in northern California had a cemetery that was having a problem. An entity was chasing another entity every night through the cemetery and across the road for two weeks straight. It is believed that the occurrence started because of a major anniversary of the event. It is not an imprint in time because it was not happening in the same place at the same time of day as the original occurrence. These events were creating a real problem with the people who lived in the area that could see paranormal activity. Several had crashed their cars trying to avoid the running spirits. Legend had it that this was a husband chasing his wife. He was reenacting the murder he committed in the 1800s. He raped and killed his wife and then subsequently had a massive heart attack and died shortly afterwards. His name is unknown at this time because the gravestone does not record it.

The sheriff heard about me. So he called and asked me to come out to take care of the problem. Now I knew that this one was going to be difficult to capture on film, never mind trying to stop them. I decided to start at the cemetery where the problems were occurring. I took several pictures and took a look around the area trying to decide on an approach to get started.

Obviously, I needed a witness on this one, so I called up a friend. She was intrigued with the sightings and drove up from the bay area the next day. Since this spirit was angry and reluctant to be photographed, it took two hours to accomplish the shoot. The entity was appearing and disappearing to me so quickly that I was not able to get a shot of him. The image of "Graveyard Spirit" (shown on the opposing page) was finally captured when, out of frustration, I set the time delay on the camera and walked away.

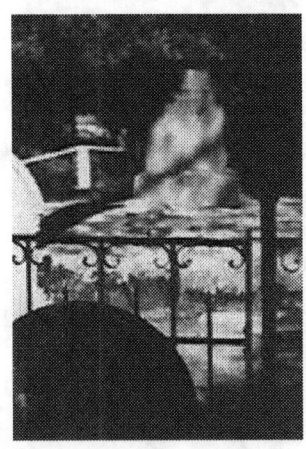

The detail of "Graveyard Spirit" on the left shows him coming out of his short boxy gravestone that was only about ten inches high. When we went back after the film had been developed, we were told that the nightly occurrences had stopped. Apparently, this spirit felt that the acknowledgement of being photographed was enough and he went on his way.

This is one of the few hostile spirits I have ever encountered.

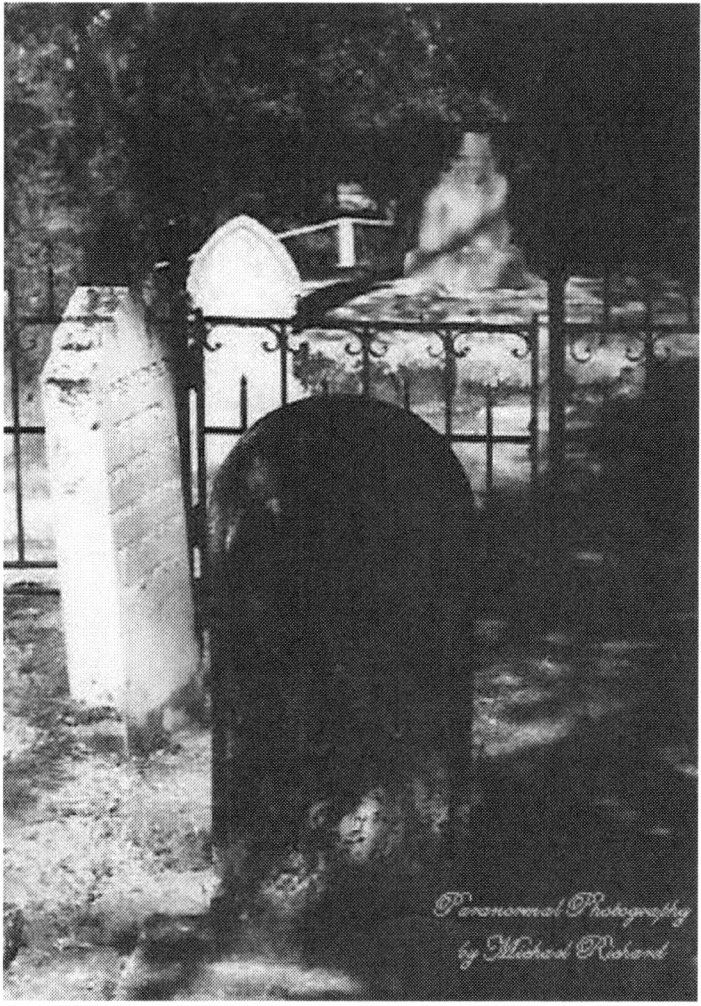

The hostel husband appears above his gravestone - "Graveyard Spirit."

The Abandoned Old Folks Home

Shortly after the cemetery incident, I was talking to a friend and he was telling me about this abandoned old folks home. It was located across the street from a little known park in a city in northern California. Patrons of the park had reported that they kept seeing movement and lights inside. There was no power to the building by this time. I found this very interesting and decided to go over with a couple of psychic friends and see what we could find.

When we arrived, we found that the building was fenced off and we could not get close to it. However, we could feel several strong spirits who were very unhappy. So, I started taking pictures with infrared film. Most frames showed nothing, however, I did get results on two shots. These results are shown on the next two pages. The "Arch of Light" was taken as one of my psychic friends told the unhappy spirits to, "Go toward the light." We believe that this is the

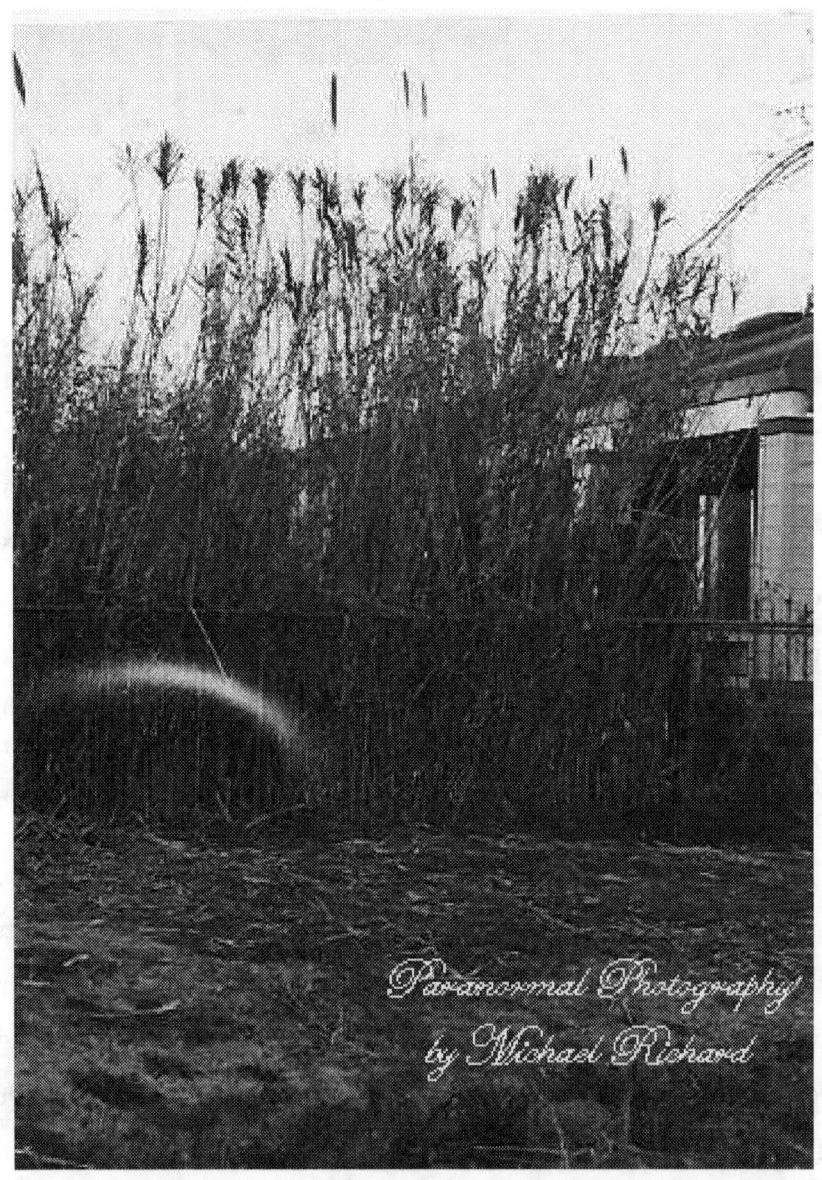

"Arch of Light" shows the arch described by near death experience survivors.

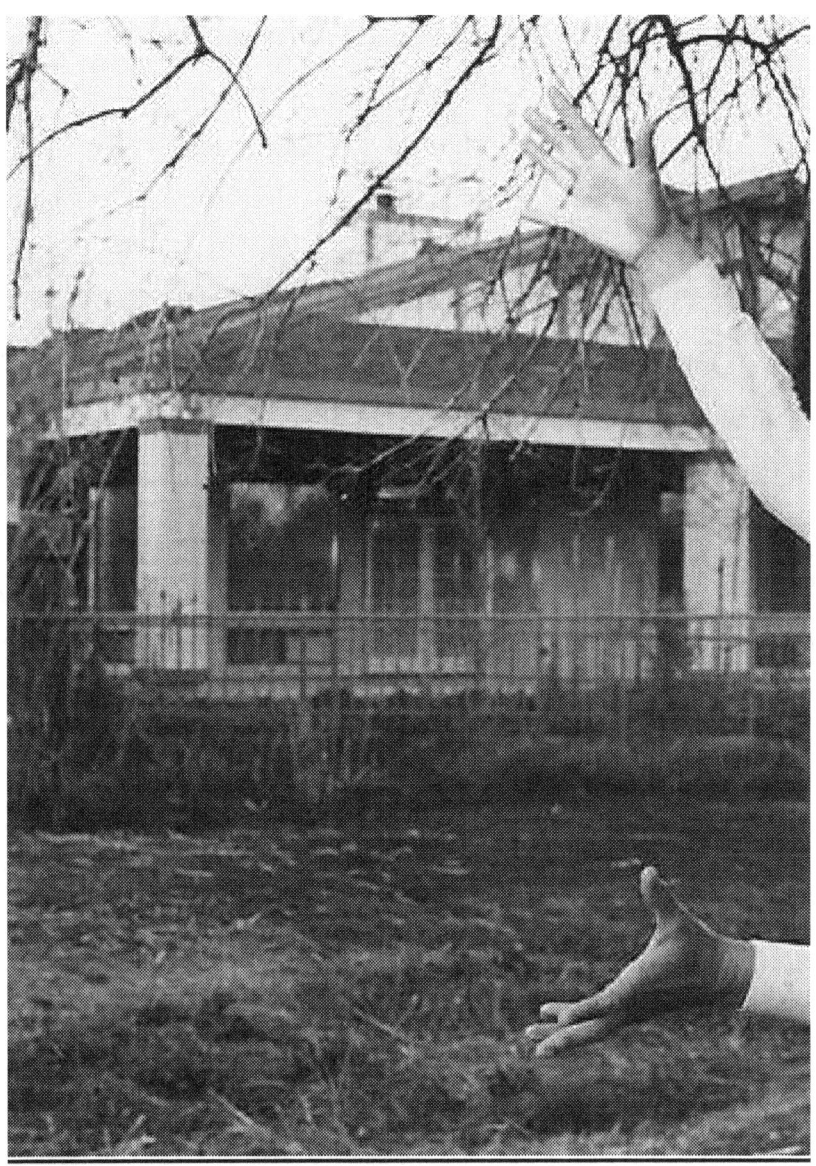

Lights and shadows in the window under porch roof

top most arch of "the tunnel of light" that is often referred to by people describing their near death experiences.

The other picture showed the lights and shadows in the windows that we could not see in this world. The day was gloomy and the window is set back into a deep porch.   However, the image did match with the reports we had gotten of the hauntings.

Only three spirits were outside and were felt to leave using the tunnel of light that my friend produced. We felt another six entities inside the building, but we were not able to help them. The State would not let us go into the building of the old folks home. To this day, we do not know exactly how many were really in the building. We did find out that the home had been closed because of suspected abuse of the patients.

Sedona, Arizona

In the summer of 1991, I took a trip to Sedona AZ. After completing the business I had in the area, I was walking around a gallery at about 10 am. I stopped to talk to a couple of people that were discussing ghosts. I gave them one of my cards and I started to leave when Frank, the gallery owner, approached me about my line of work. He told me about some Anasazi ruins that were not generally known to the public. He thought they might produce some interesting results. Frank gave me detailed directions to this site.

Within an hour, I had gathered my things and checked out of my hotel. I ate lunch and then headed up to the ruins. When I arrived at about one that afternoon, I was amazed to feel not one spirit, but two waiting for me and vying for my attention. The conditions there were excellent. It was about 80 degrees with the sun behind me. It was a clear day, so the sun glowed into the ruins.

I waited for some tourist to leave the area. Then, I set up my tripod near the strongest entity first, later to be known as "Anasazi Man." He was posing for me in a room connected to a Kiva type pit. As is common in daylight for me, I could see him when I looked thru the lens on the camera.

This first spirit wanted to send his message, so the image known as "Anasazi Man" shows an incredible amount of detail for this kind of photography. Everything in this photograph (on page 44) is the image of the spirit and his spirit energy. His head starts in the upper right side of the frame showing one eye and a partial face mask. In the middle of the frame, his shield and abdomen are visible. He is wearing a leather skirt low on his abdomen in the lower left of the frame. To help some people see the image of the "Anasazi", my wife used some watercolors to emphasize the figure. This second version is known as "Anasazi Man – Colorized" seen on page 45.

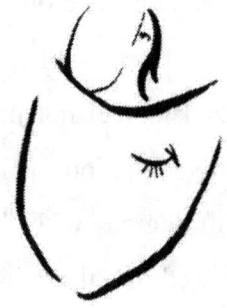

The amount of detail and rarity of the image of "Anasazi Man" has made it the most asked about photograph in my collection. It is generally considered my signature piece. For this reason, my wife and I decided to base our logo (shown in the detail on the left) on the image of the "Anasazi Man" (shown below.)

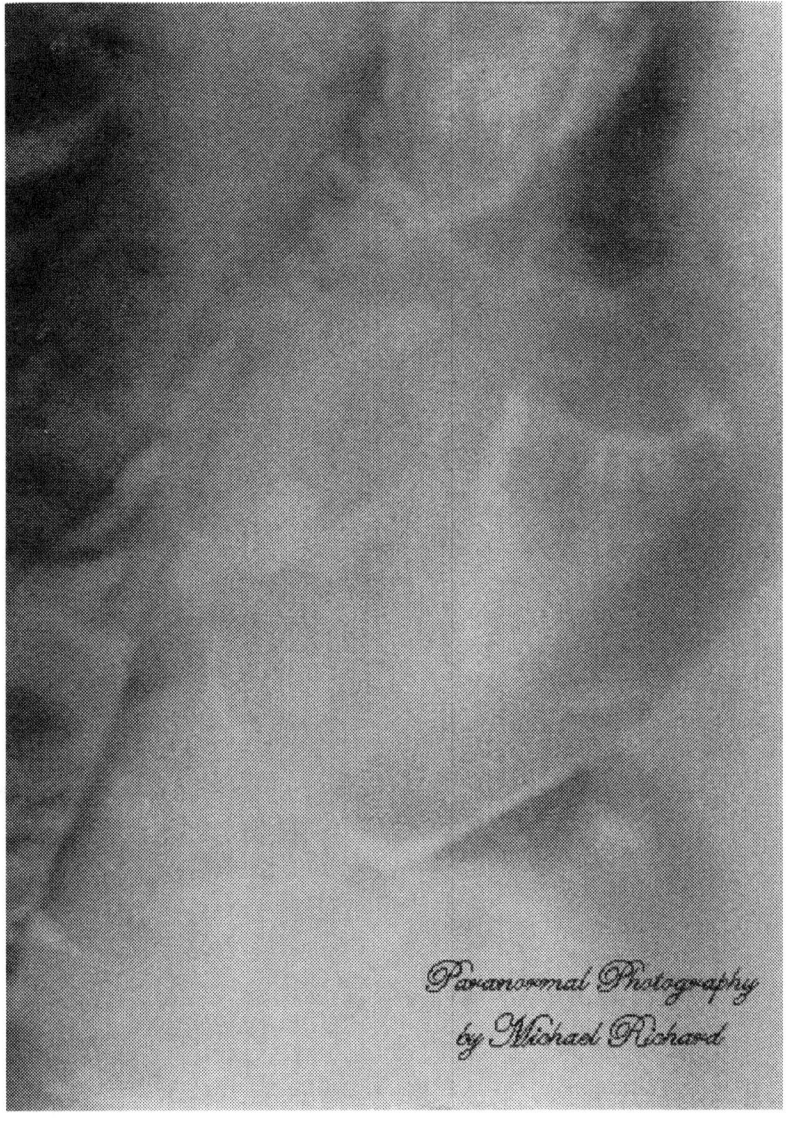

The entire frame shows the spirit and spirit energy of "Anasazi Man."

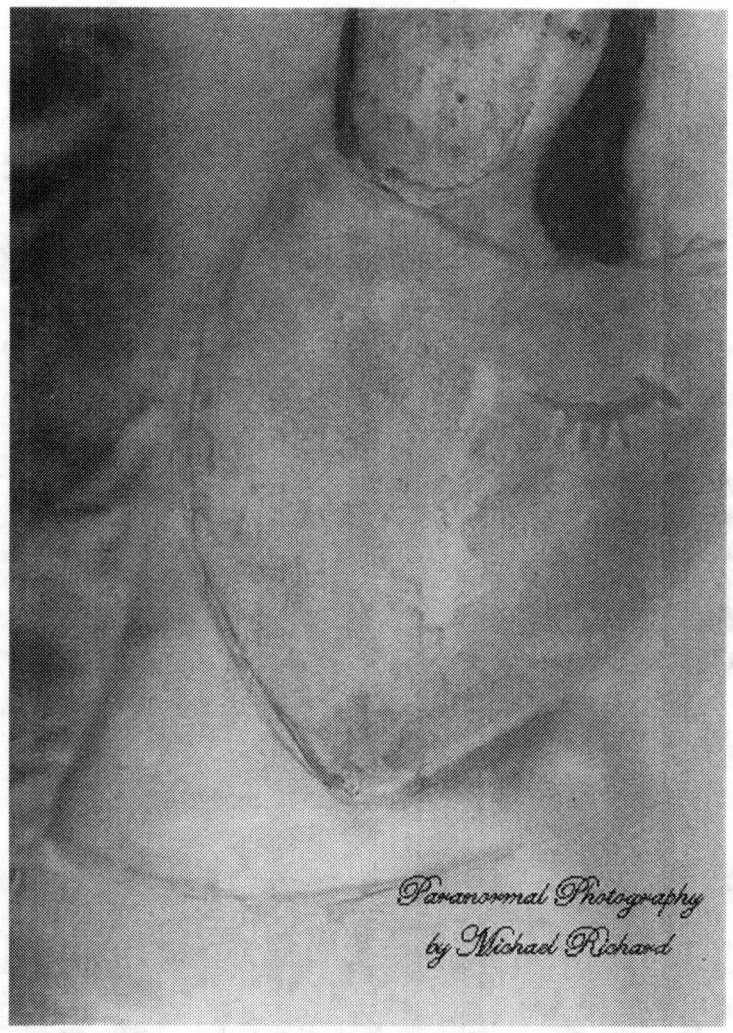

"Anasazi Man – Colorized" shows the spirit more clearly.

The next entity was posing about 10 feet away outside of a rock wall. This photograph also shows only spirits and spirit

energy. The face on the left in the lower two-thirds of the frame is
the image that we call "Rocky Spirit" (seen below.)

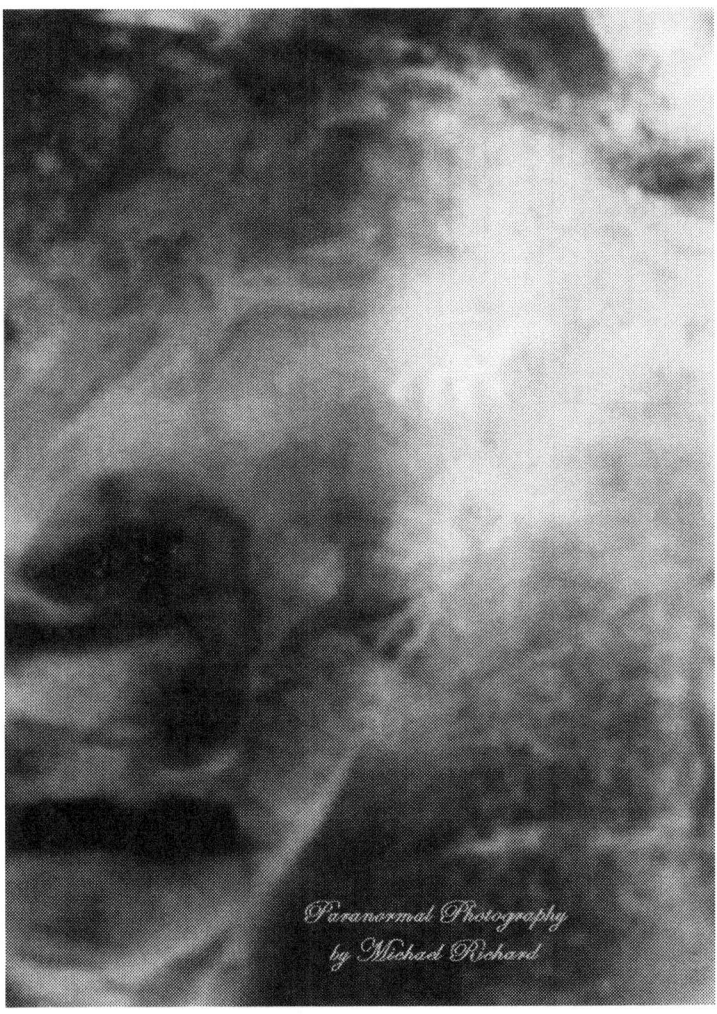

"Rocky Spirit" shows multiple spirits and spirit energy.

I finished off the roll of film checking for any other paranormal activity. The entities were so eager to be photographed that I was done within thirty minutes. These two pages show two more images of spirits that I got that day.

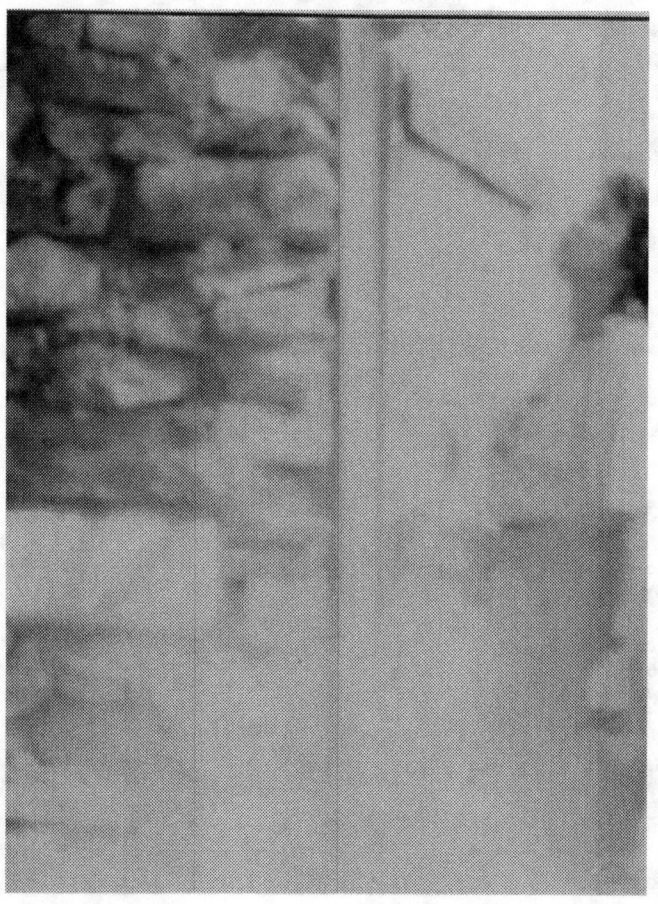

This shows the spirit energy glowing at the bottom.

The bearded face is a third down the image and slightly to the right of center. The glow under the face is the body of the spirit.

After completing my shoot, I left Sedona and went home to Colorado. Upon my return, I immediately sent my film to our local lab. I received the results a week later. Because the first two entities wanted to send their messages, each image shows an incredible amount of detail for this kind of photography. The third image has just some spirit energy visible. The last image is very faint, but it still shows a lot of detail. Some people think this one looks a lot like Jesus.

Within a week of taking these photographs the ruins collapsed. That was the last time the "Anasazi Man" spirit was felt in the area. Subsequent research and discussion with some archeologists located out of Cortez, Colorado, determined that the image is most likely of a spirit from the Anasazi culture.

Mesa Verde, Colorado

I was living in Colorado Springs, Colorado in 1994. That summer we decided to go to Durango, Colorado for vacation and do the tourist thing. While we were there, we took day trips to the Mesa Verde Ruins between Durango and Cortez, Colorado and the Aztec Ruins in Aztec, New Mexico.

In Mesa Verde National Park, we went to Spruce Tree ruins and we took the tour of Cliff Palace ruins. Tourist can walk to Spruce Tree ruins without a ranger guide. I shot a roll of film at Spruce Tree, but when it was processed it came back blank. At least one of the spirits there did not want to show up on film and zapped the whole roll.

The roll of film I shot during the guided tour of Cliff Palace produced several results. Eight frames showed bars of spirit energy. These ruins are set back in the cliff and there is no reflective or direct light around the ruins themselves.

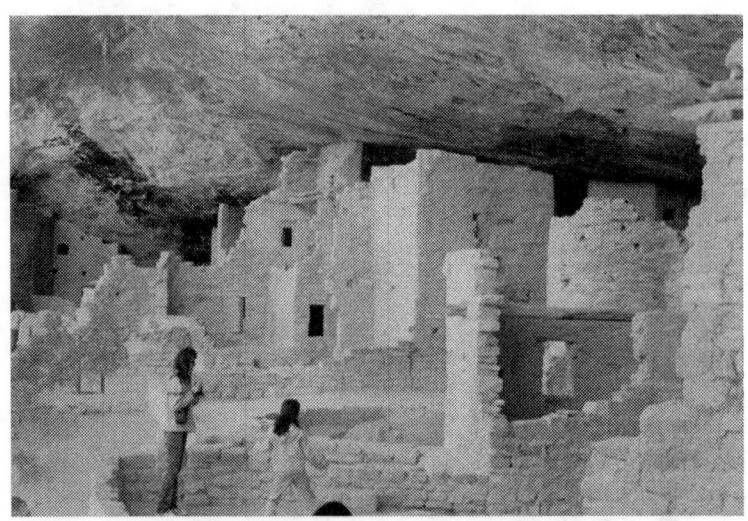

Spruce Tree Ruins taken at a later date with regular film.

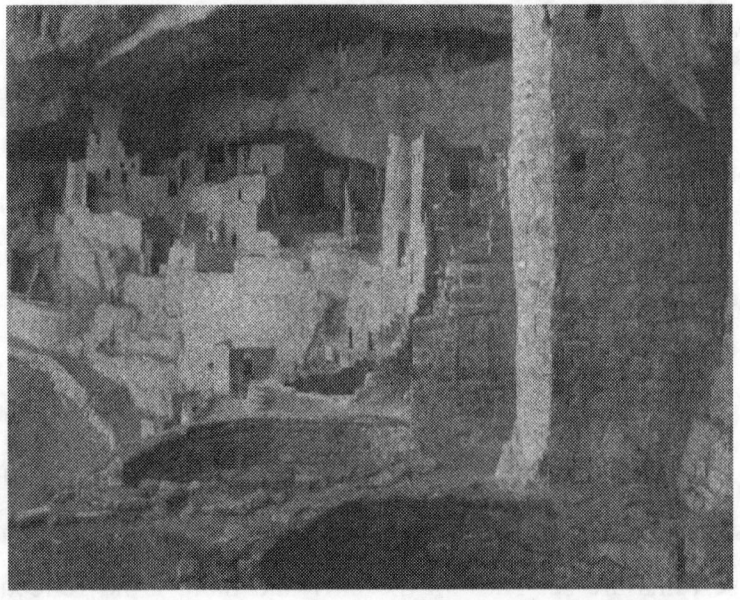

Cliff Palace Ruins taken at a later date with a digital camera.

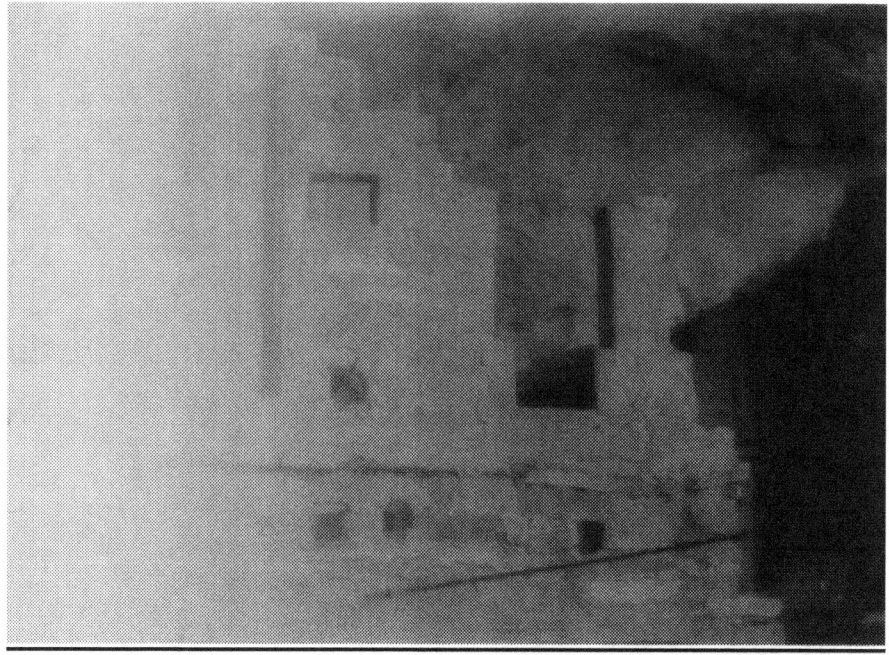

Spirit energy is located on the left.

The image that we call "Kiva Light" (seen on page 55) is the best of the spirit energy shots. This shot was taken pointed down into the kiva, which was in heavy shadows.

The first photograph you see on page 56, shows a tourist crouching in an alcove behind a kiva next to the back wall of the cliff. When I went back there and took a shot, I got the image that we call "Spirited Rock" (the second image seen on page 56.)

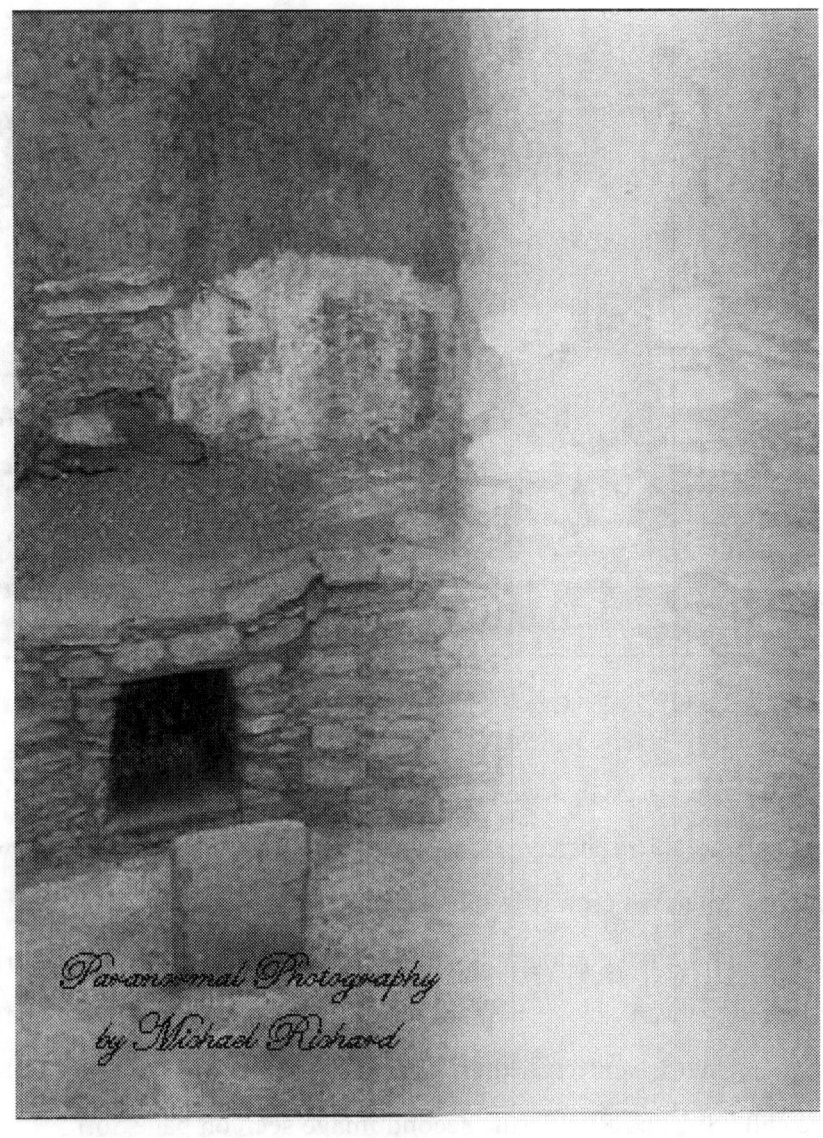

"Kiva Light" was taken pointed down into the heavily shadowed kiva.

The spirit energy bar is located on the right.

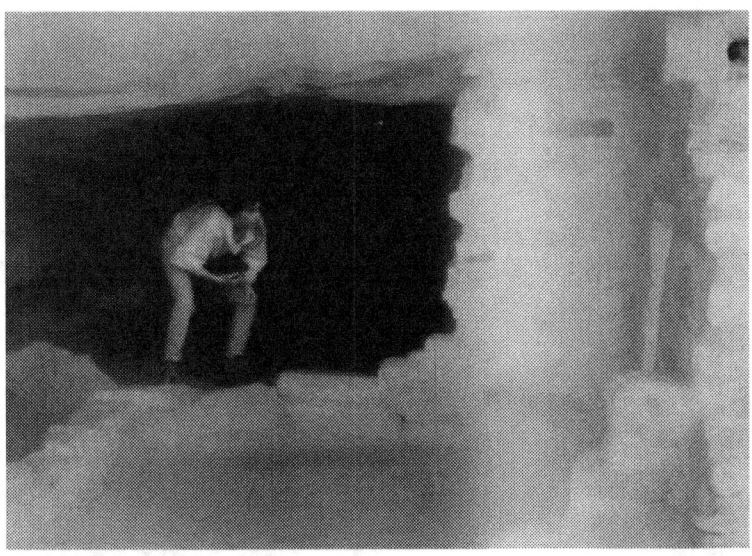

Above a tourist is seen crouching in an alcove with a weak spirit energy on the right.
"Spirited Rock" (below) shows an intense spirit energy in the bottom half of this shot taken
with the camera pointed at the back of the alcove wall.

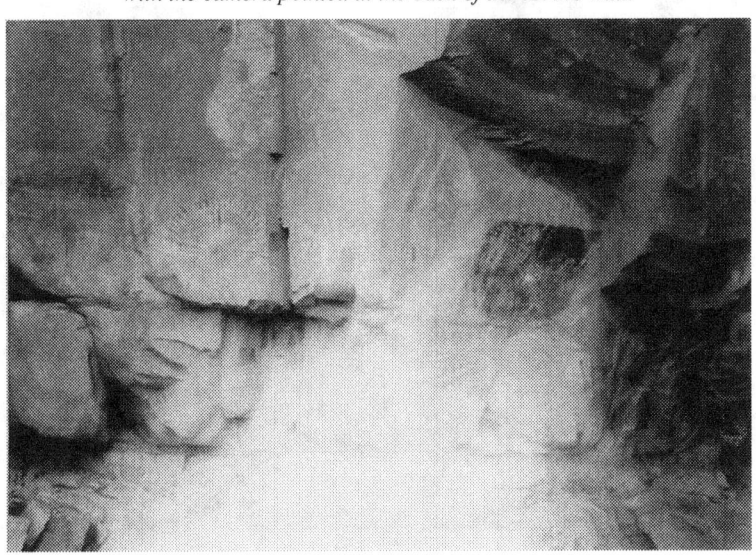

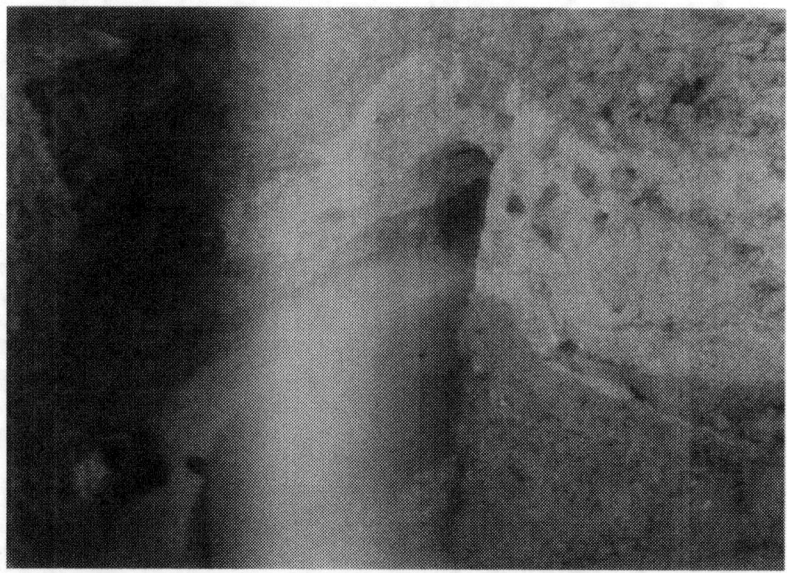

Both of these images are inside kivas and show spirit energy in the middle of the frame.

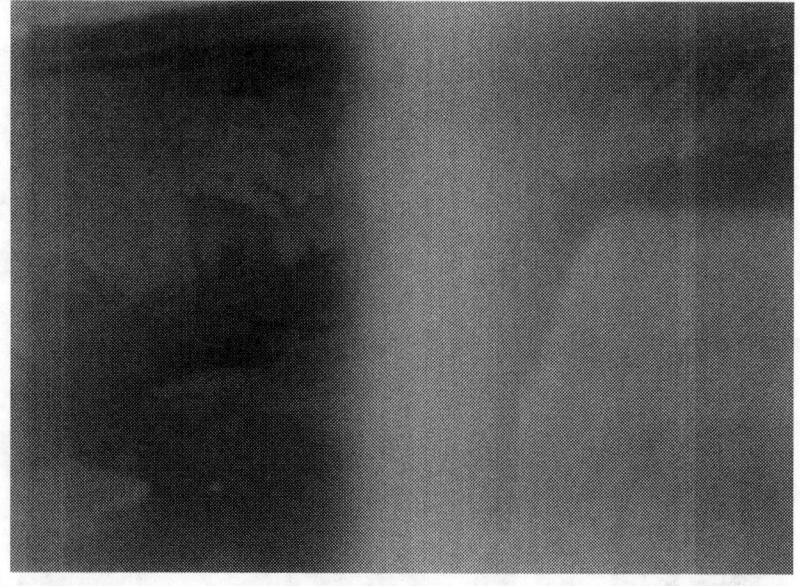

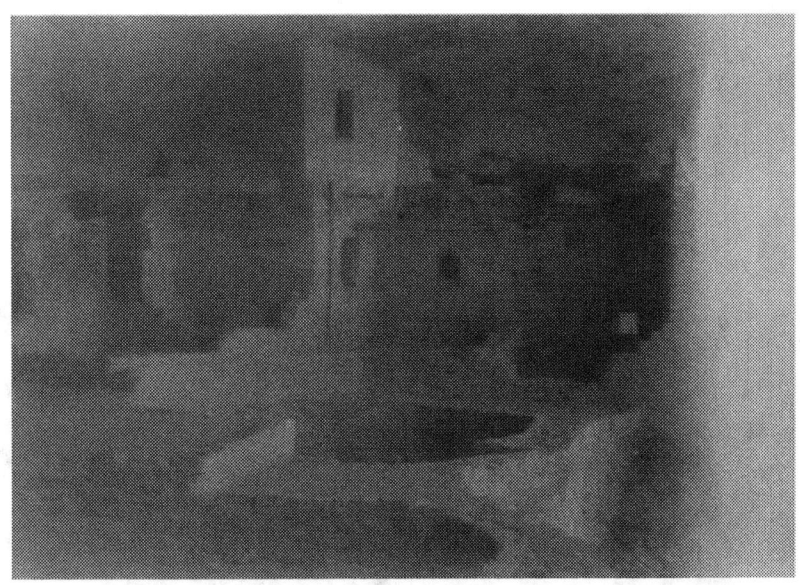

Above the spirit energy is located on the right. Below the spirit energy is in the middle.

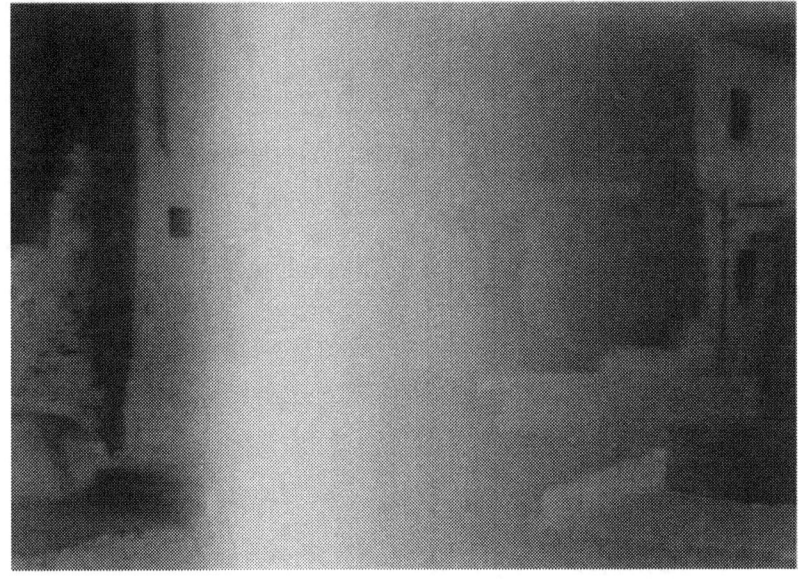

The path that leads out of Cliff Palace runs along the cliff wall for a short distance. I took the next two shots just feet from the bottom of the stone steps leading up the cliff wall back to the parking lot.

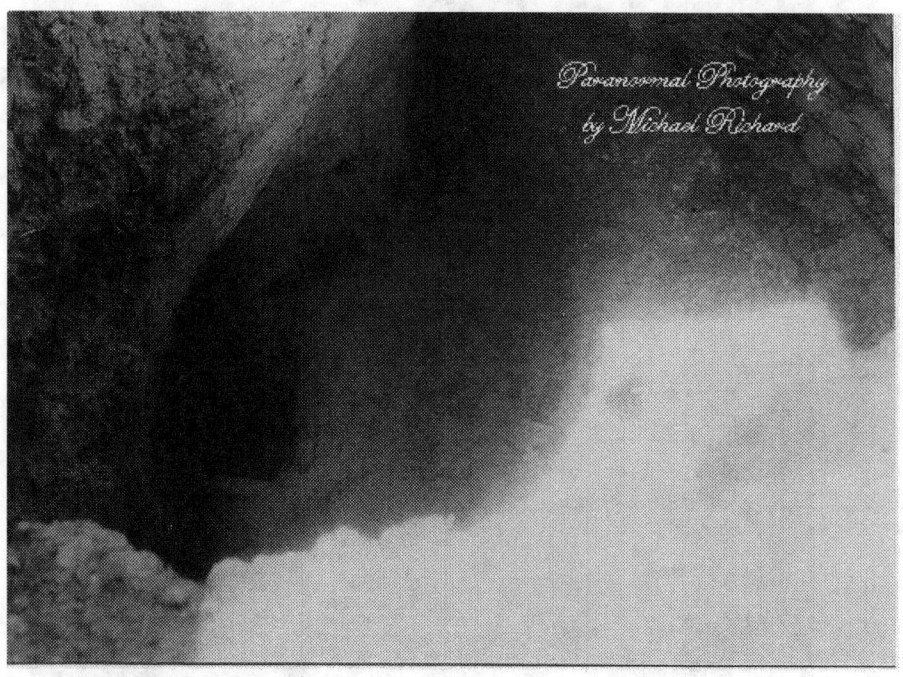

"Healing Rock" shows the rock glowing with its healing powers.

The image we call "Healing Rock" (shown above) is of a large rectangular boulder at the bottom of the steps. This rock's powers have been known for decades. The healing energy that this rock produces shows up as a glowing white light on the infrared film. Just to the left of "Healing Rock" I captured this other image that shows spirit energy on the left.

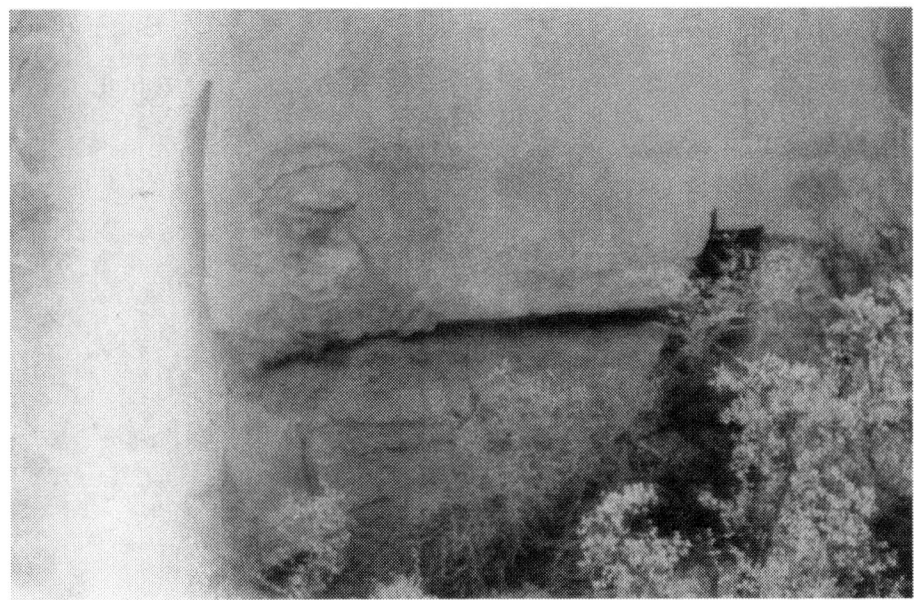

The spirit energy is seen on the left.

We made another excursion the next day to the Aztec Ruins National Park in Aztec, New Mexico, just south of the Colorado border. The photographic results from this trip were disappointing in comparison to Mesa Verde. We include these results here because they are close to Mesa Verde and represent another section of the Chacoan culture.

We only got two images that day with spirit energy bars in them. One image, however, got ruined in a flood. The remaining image shows one strong spirit, vertically on the right, and a fainter one vertically in the middle. It also shows one horizontally along the bottom connecting the other two.

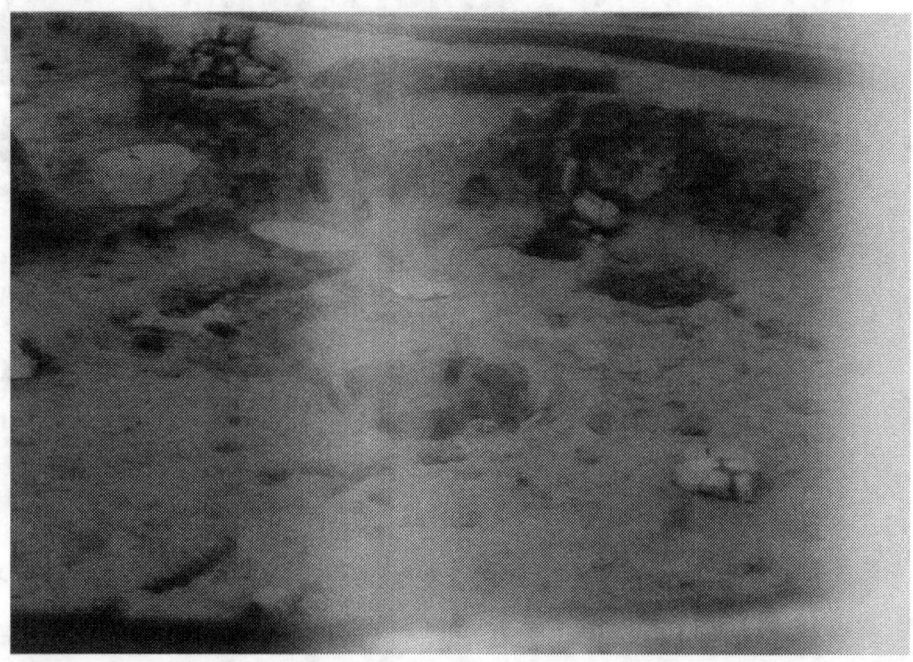

This Aztec ruins kiva shows three spirit energy bars.

Bodie, California

In the spring of 2003, we were visiting relatives, John and Judy Whitaker, in Bishop, CA. We were discussing things to do in the area. They mentioned a cool ghost town close by called Bodie. John called to

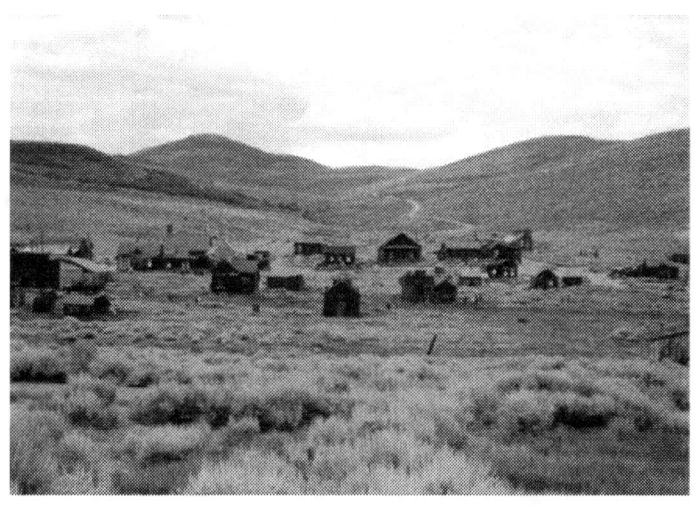

Bodie, California

see if the road was open yet for the season. It was, so all four of us went out to see what we could find.

John is also into photography. He finds what I can get on film fascinating and wanted to see if he could get anything like mine. He did in this shot (on the facing page) of a window in one of the buildings. In the lower right corner of the bottom left pane of this window, there appears to be a couple of very faint screaming or anguished faces. It is difficult to see when printed in this book. So in the detail on page 65, I have not only blown it up, I have lightened the image to make it more visible in this printing. John's shot was actually the only figure shot we got that day.

I got two images myself (shown on page 66.) The first shows focus distortion and movement. The second shows an energy spirit.

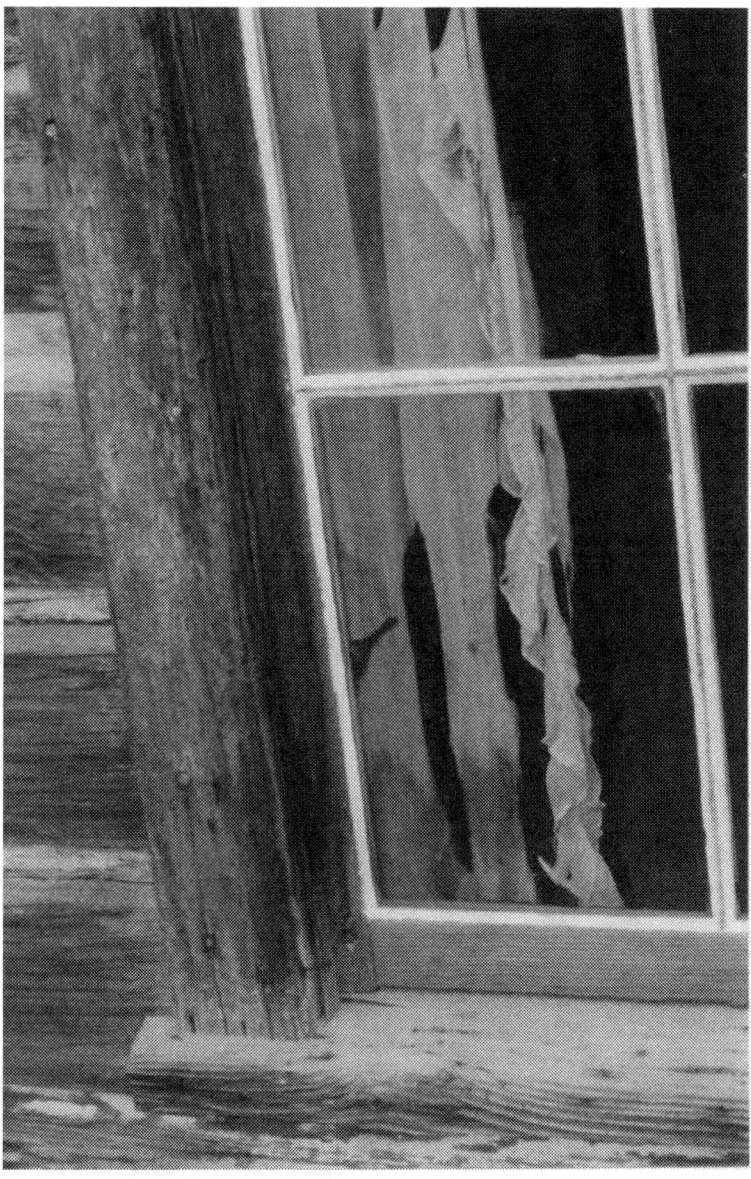

Window shot by John Whitaker with regular film.

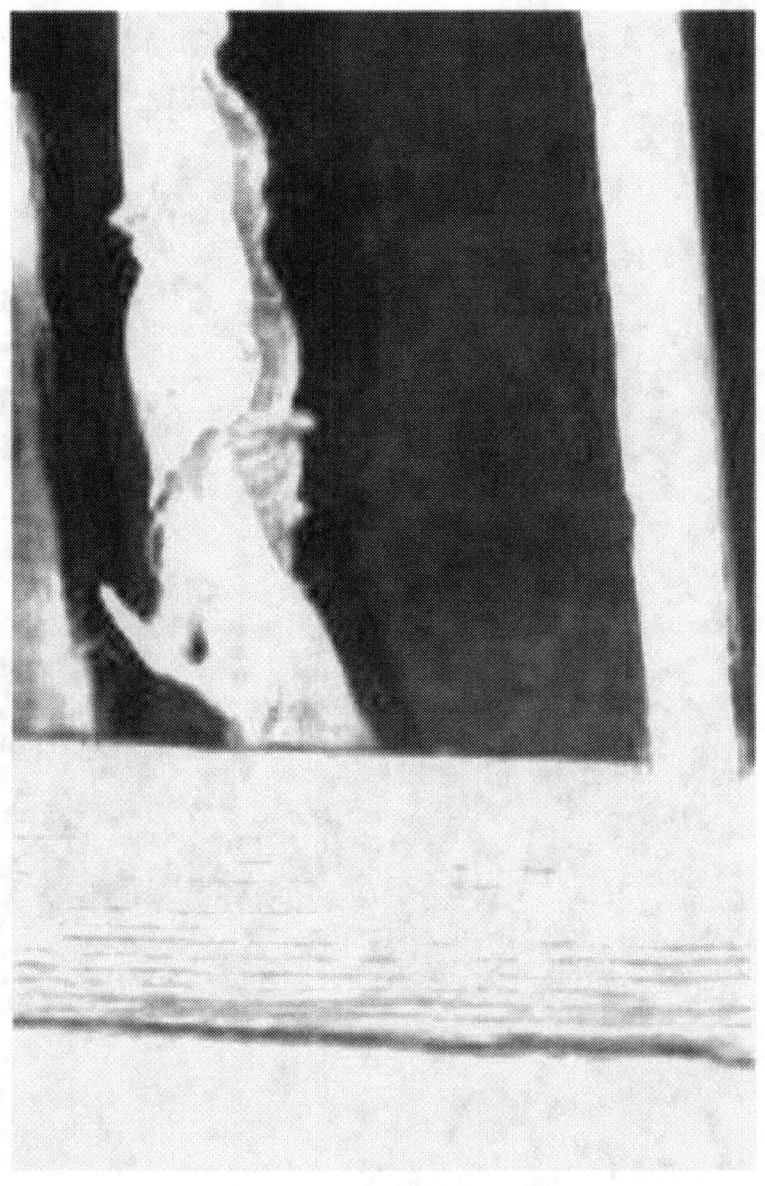

Detail of lower right of window, shows two faces in bottom of window pane.

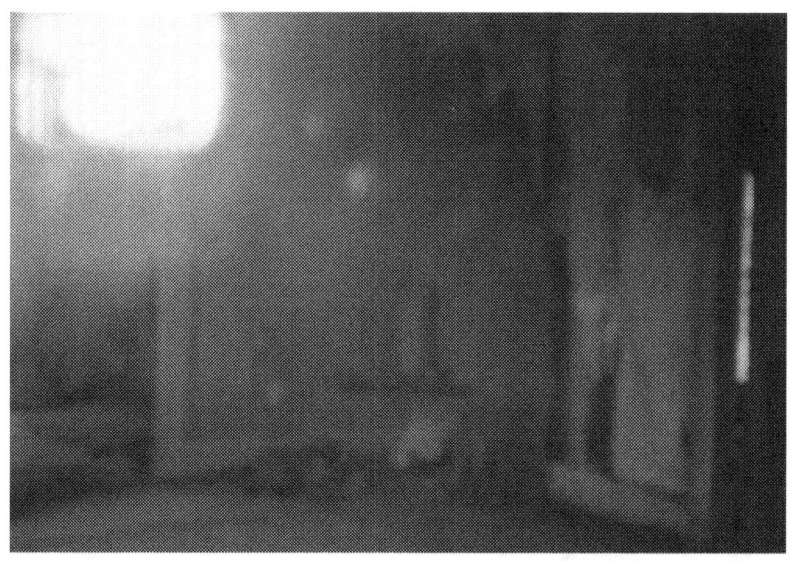

The image above was taken in living quarters and shows the distortion of the focus.
The image below shows spirit energy in the upper left of the frame.

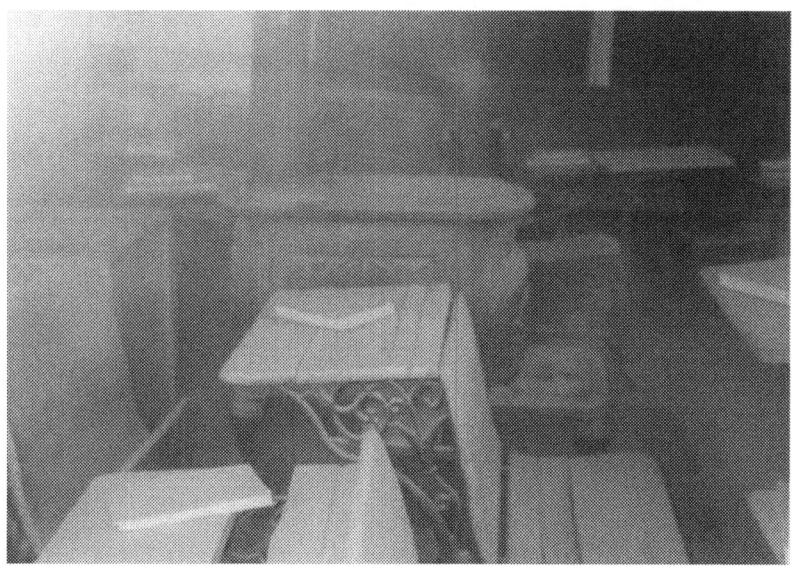

St. James Hotel

The St. James Hotel in Cimarron, New Mexico is considered to be one of the most haunted hotels in the US. There are very few guests who spend the night there that do not have stories to tell in the morning! If you are seeking ghost activity this is the place to stay.

We went there in the winter of 2005. The owner was pleased to see us and gave us a guided tour. He even opened the locked

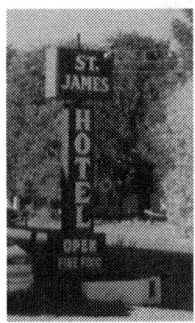 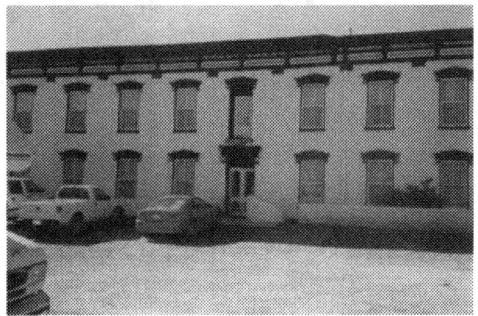

James Hotel, Cimarron, New Mexico.

room where their most cantankerous spirit resided.

To placate this spirit, they would place a fresh bottle of whiskey in the room weekly. The next week the bottle would always be empty. This did have the affect of keeping the spirit happy and in that room. We could feel his presence, but he did not want to be photographed.

Other spirits residing in the hotel were more accommodating, such as this spirit in the hotel's "Poker Room." There was a window on the other side of the room. However, the blinds were closed. This photo was taken with regular film by Susan.

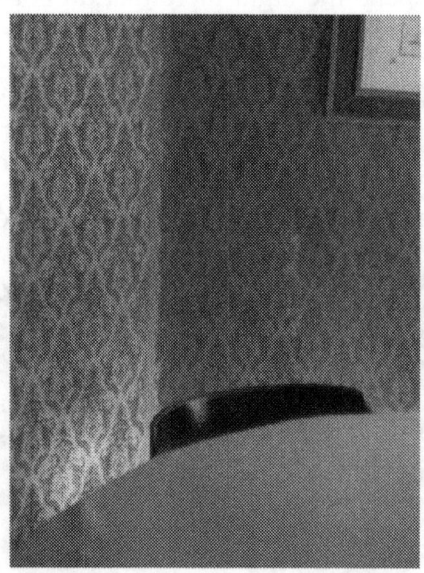

The spirit energy in this image is seen above the table edge to the left of the chair.

These two photographs show how spirits can sometimes affect film strangely. They were taken with high speed film. The upper part of each photograph shows movement.

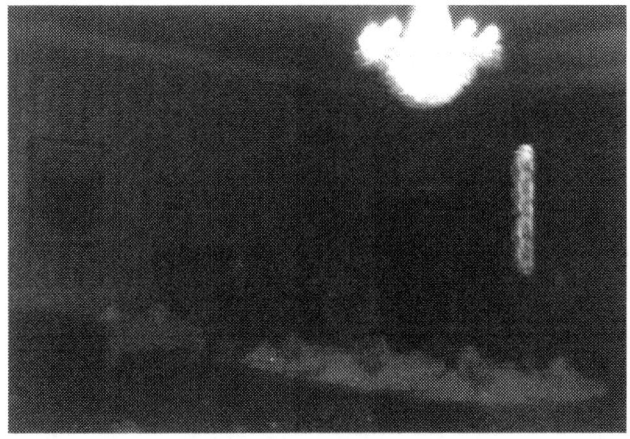

The left side of the dinning room above is in focus.
Below the hallway is in focus on the bottom of the photograph.

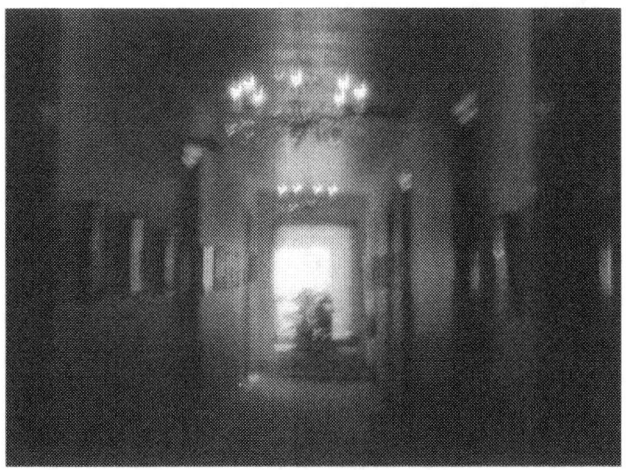

Private Homes

On a vacation in 1987, I went to a metaphysical fair in Sedona, Arizona. I met Michael Big Bear when he did a card reading for me. Michael Big Bear is a Cherokee medicine man. During the reading, Big Bear got a message about my photography and asked me to explain it to him. We agreed to meet later for lunch to get better acquainted and for a more detailed discussion on my photography. After which, we ended up at his house to do a ceremony to bring me into his protective circle.

Later that week we went out to the medicine wheel he had built along a hiking trail. At the medicine wheel we ran into Reba and her daughter performing a ceremony. I started taking pictures of their ceremony, the medicine wheel and the area. Reba wanted to know what I was doing. So I told her. At which point she said, "Well that does it, you have to come to my house."

Later that day we had a Bar-B-Que at her house. While everyone was outside and the house was dark and empty, I took some photographs with infrared film from the back patio. When I was done, Reba took the film to a lab she knew that could develop specialized film overnight. The next morning, I picked up the photographs and we met up for breakfast to discuss the results. The photographs showed lights, figures and movement.

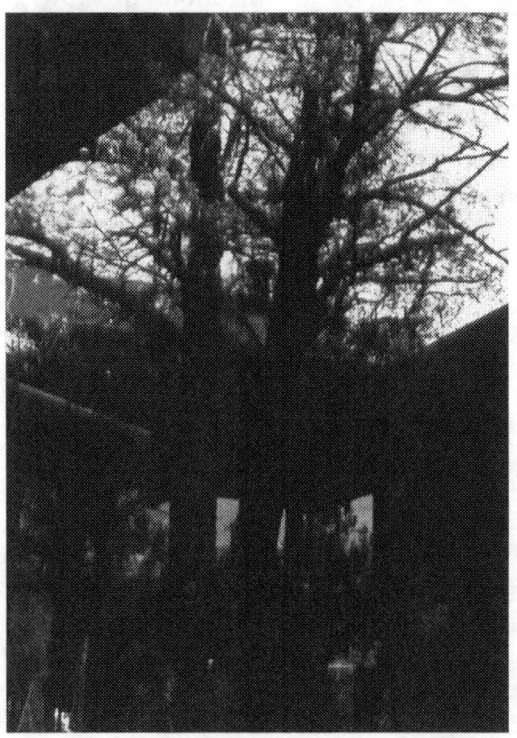

You can see a face in the lower left corner.

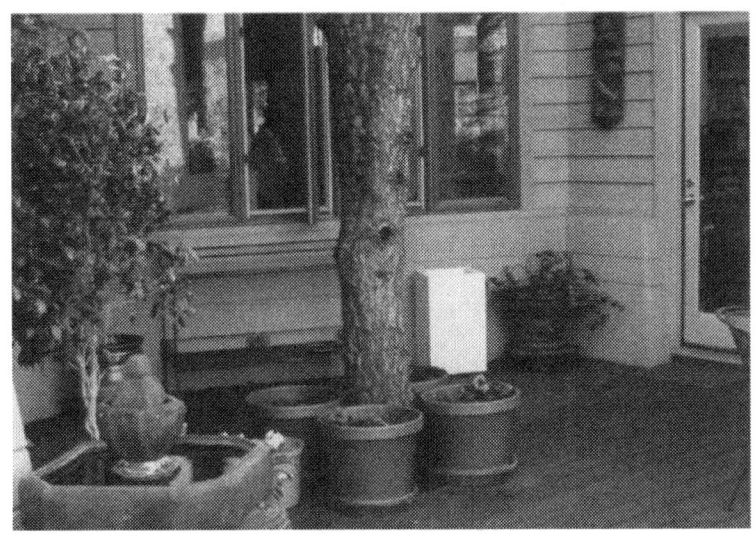

In the upper picture there is a figure behind the open window
when no one was inside the house.

In the lower picture there was no mirror or window behind the open window.

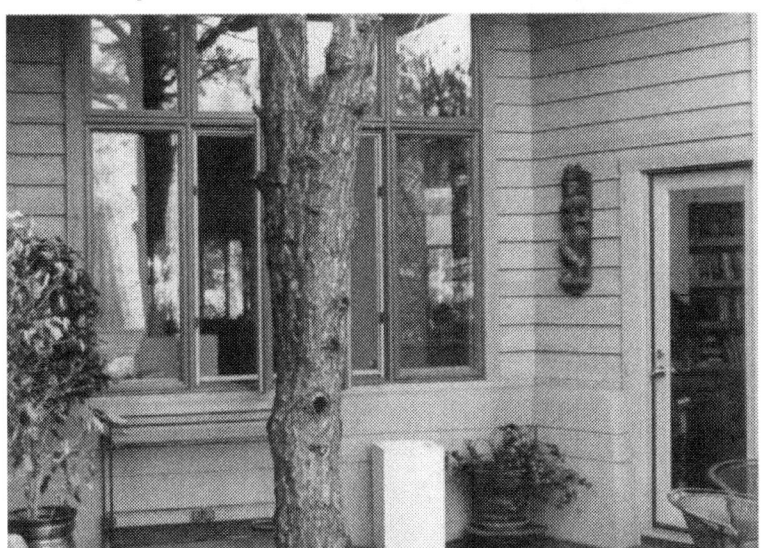

In Sacramento, California in 1986, the mother of a friend of mine was into Wicca (a religion that is based on the earth and nature including any powers associated with them.) She stated that she could feel several spirits within her home and wanted me to see what I could get on film. I got this picture of her on the opposite page with a shaft of light that starts outside the window, crosses over her right ear and along her back.

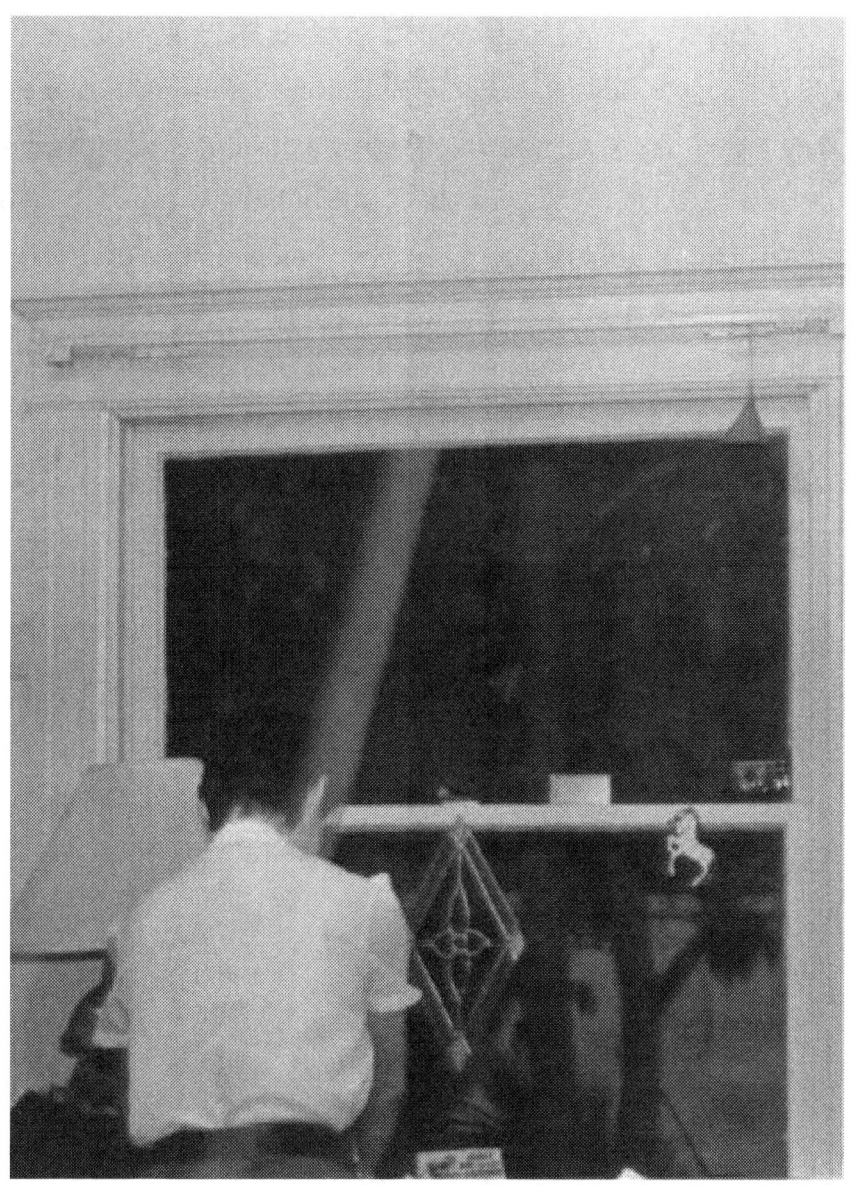

Light shaft through the window.

During a metaphysical show in Austin, Texas in March of 2004, a couple came up to the booth while I was taking a break. They talked to my stepson Joel for a while and then expressed an interest in talking to me personally. Joel told them that I would be back in another 10 minutes. They went on to see more of the show and came back about an hour later. The man stated that his first wife had died in their home. He was now remarried and strange things had started happening. He requested a photo shoot.

A few days later, after the show had ended, I went over to his house. I could feel the former wife's presence. So we took all the information from them and started the shoot. We got one possible image.

These pictures are from Susan's camera using regular film. The first shot shows the frame before the photograph with spirit distortion. The distortion shows the interference the entity caused on the focus of the image. The focus was the same for both. The frame after is also clearly focused.

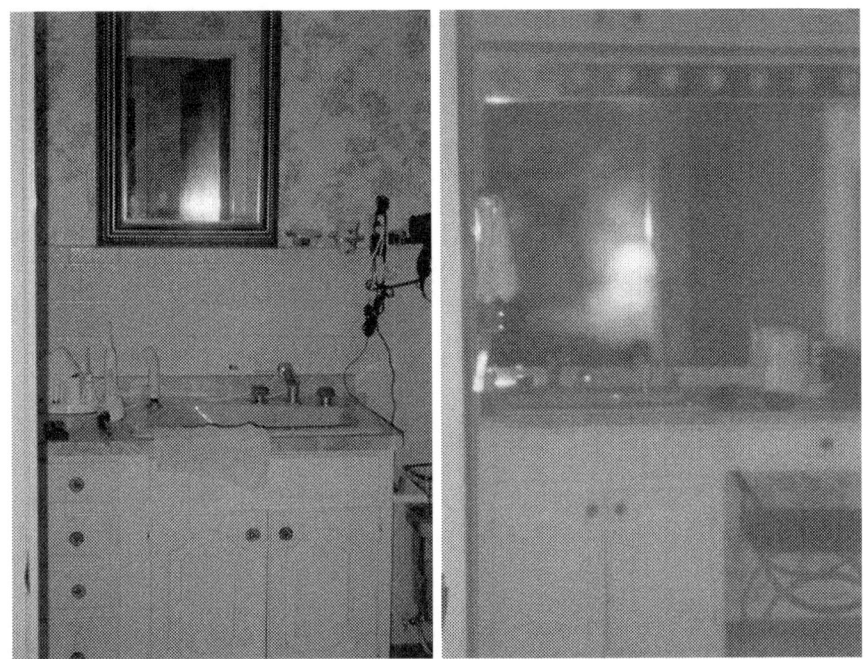

These frames show how some spirits interfere with the focus of your shot.

George Nakata

I first met George at a metaphysical fair outside of Colorado Springs, Colorado in 1993. The producers of the fair had asked me to take some pictures of the proceedings. While I was walking around, I observed how George was working on people using healing energy. I started taking pictures of him. When he asked me what I was doing, I explained who I am and what I do. I picked up one of his business cards and told him I would contact him when I got the photographs back from the lab. A week later, I called George and made an appointment to meet with him.

George Nakata is an energy worker. He heals, or at least eases, people's "dis-ease." When I showed him the photographs I took that day, he cried. He told me that now he can show people what he feels and sees himself when he works with people. His favorite image was the one showing a cone of light radiating down on him while he was working. Since that day, George and I have become good friends. I have taken pictures of several more sessions that he has done.

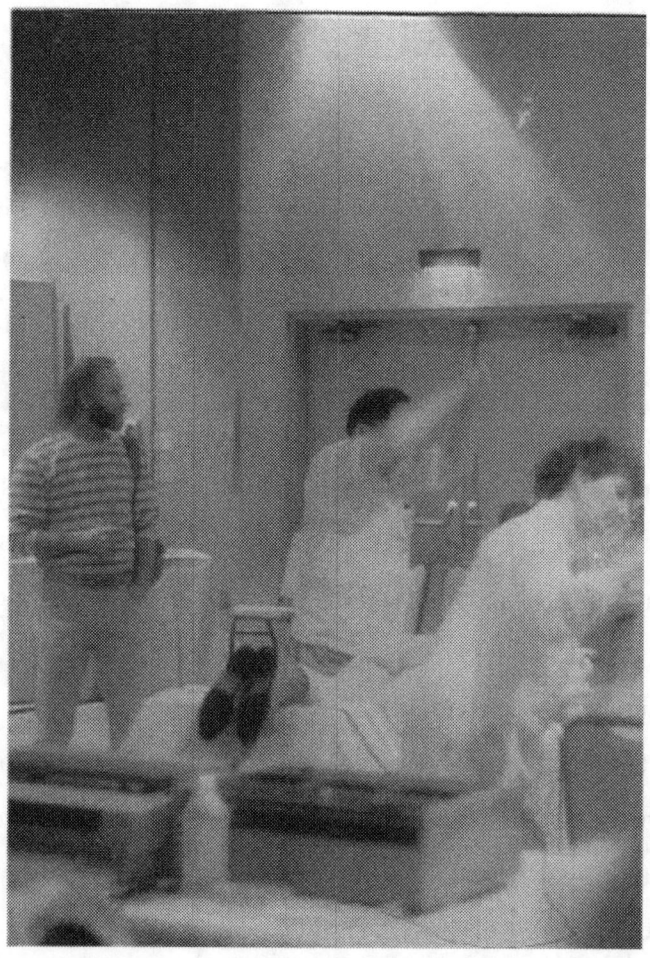

There was no light source directly above George

Six months later, at a metaphysical fair in Denver, Colorado.
George conducted an energy demonstration. He chose a woman
from the audience who seemed very interested in his work. George
asked the woman if she had any physical problems. She stated that
she had some back problems. He had her hold up a round steel plate
against her chest. He hit it with a hammer and she felt nothing.

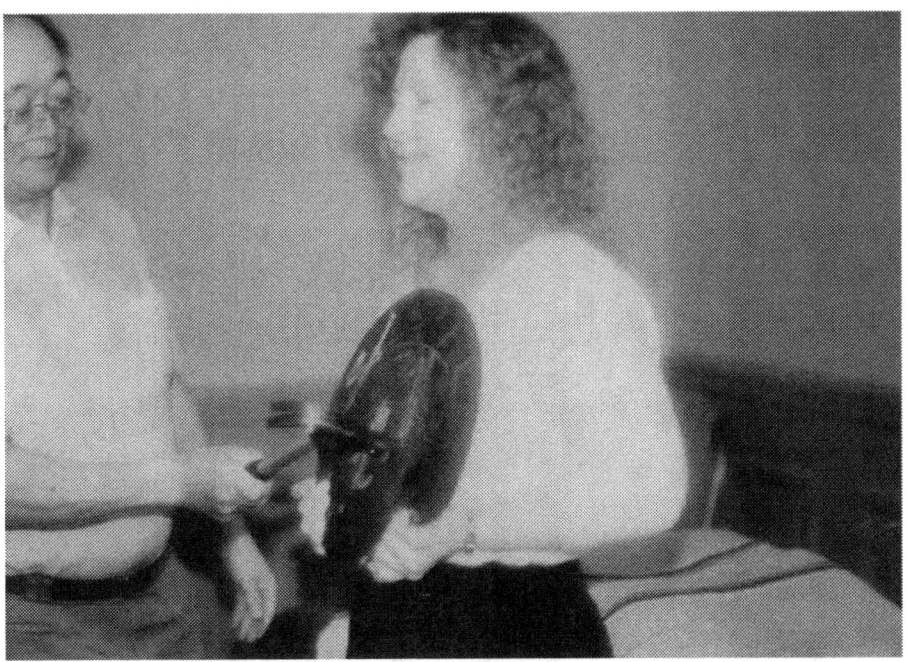

George hits the metal plate with his hammer and nothing happens.

However, when George hit the plate with his fist, she felt the

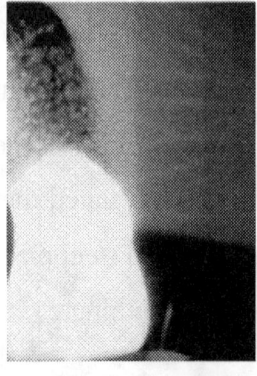

energy pass through her and bounce off of the wall behind (see detail to the right). In the final picture that I got you can see the lines of energy radiating out from her head and back centering at her neck. She stated after the demonstration, that her back felt much better.

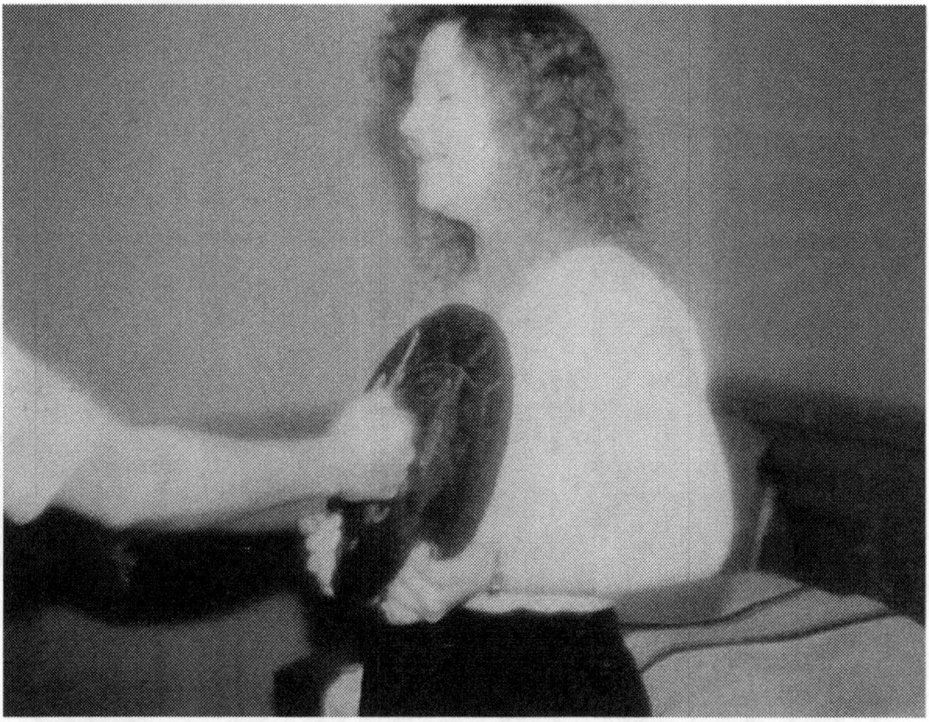

George hits the metal plated with his fist and shows lines of energy bouncing between her and the wall.

During one session at George's house, he had several people gathered for a series of healing sessions. About twenty minutes after I had set up, I started to feel a spirit that wanted to send a message. He was using George's energy to show up in the shot. We call this image "Ghost in Sink" and it is shown on page 87.

While George was engulfed in his white light, the spirit positioned himself behind George, but still within the focal length of the shot. This put him coming out of George's kitchen sink. In this

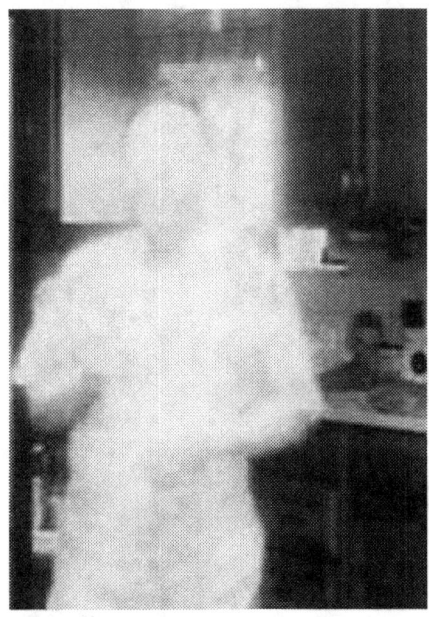

detail shot you can see him to the right of George's elbow and partially behind the canister. It also enabled the shot to include this spirit's wife to whom he was trying to send the message. I sent the film to the lab the next day.   A week later when I received the results, I contacted everybody that was there that day. We arranged to all meet two weeks later. During the discussions, the question of who this spirit is/was came up. This is when his wife told us that her husband had died six months before the meeting. She showed us a picture

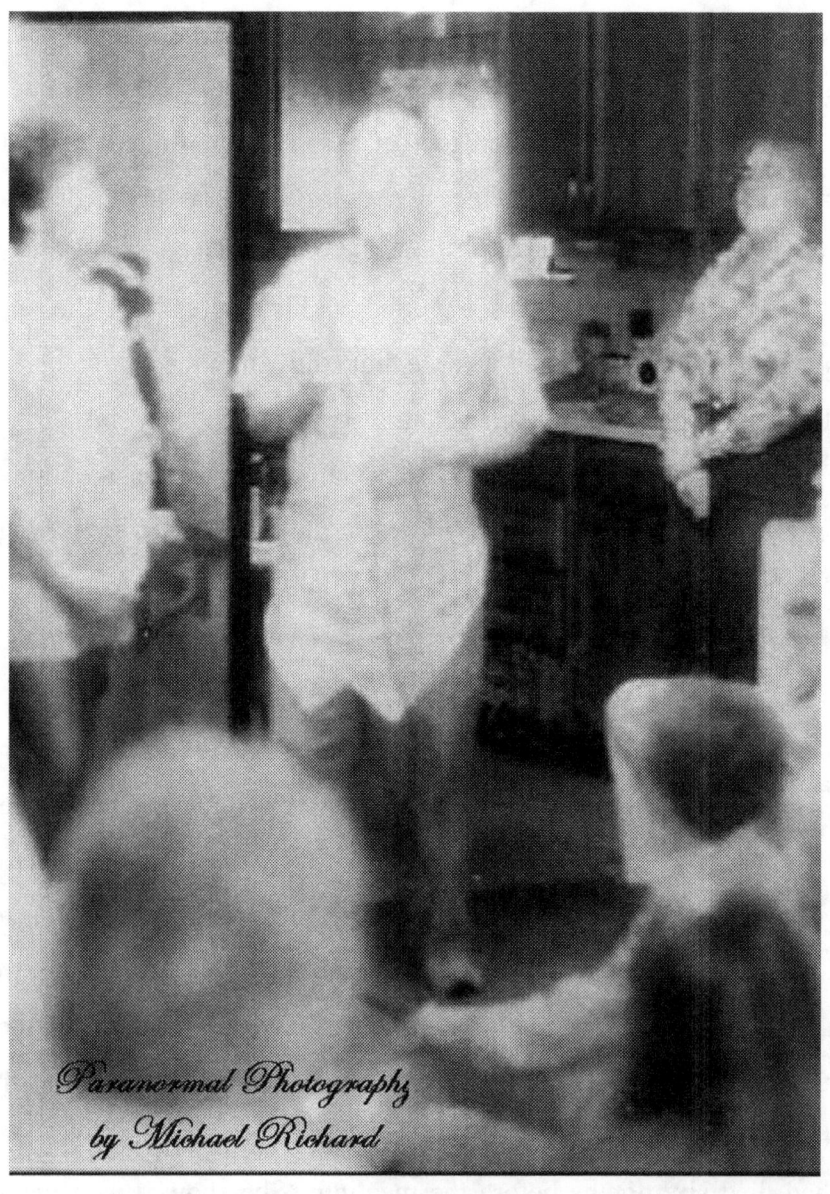

"Ghost in Sink"

that she had in her wallet and it was clearly the same man.

Several years later I produced a metaphysical show in Durango, Colorado. George was working on a woman with lower back pain. In this photograph you can see him and the woman's lower back engulfed in white light. Six months later I came across this woman and she stated that she still had no back pain.

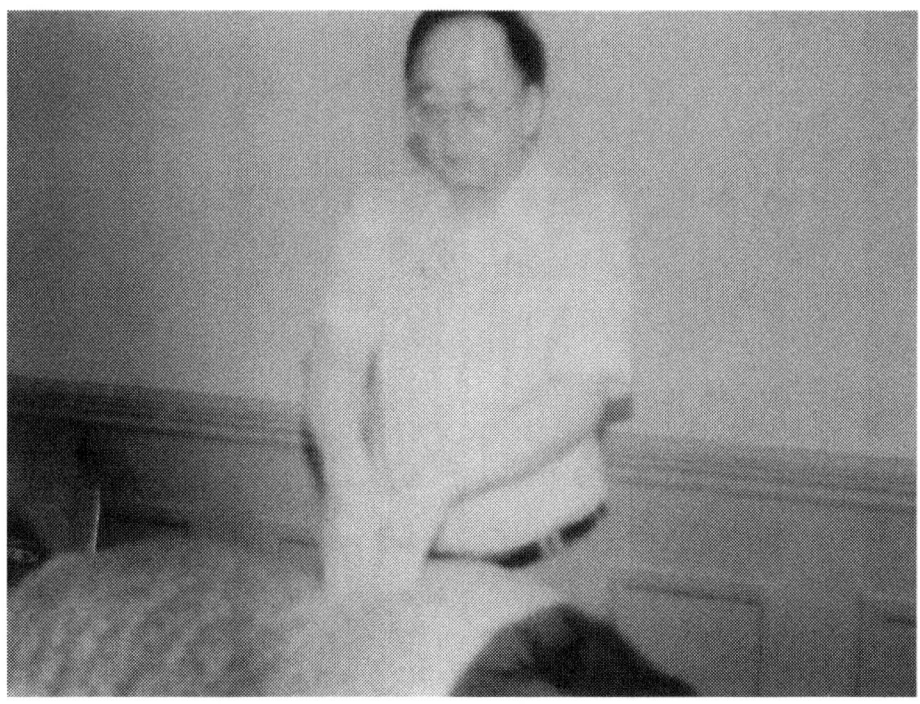

George's hands are glowing and envelope this women's lower back.

Psychics

L et's talk about what "psychic" means. There are many different abilities that fall into this category. Most clairvoyants have the ability to "check in" in limited ways. Some can get readings or messages only through other means such as tarot cards or physical touch. Others get readings and messages through one on one contact with people. And then, some people only receive these things through dreams or channeling. I have known psychics who were intuitive for certain areas such as medical diagnoses or lost items. I have known several that can tap multiple accesses, but some cannot. It is possible for psychics to grow in their abilities, but it usually takes time and effort. My point is just because someone says that they are psychic doesn't mean that they have the ability to do it all! You need to trust your instincts.

To be clear, I will use this time to explain my abilities. As I said before, I started out just seeing auras after my drowning experience. Next, a year later, I started to see ghosts as glowing white figures. Several years later, I started to see more detailed images. I was in my twenties before I started hearing messages from the other side. These messages are only personal messages from a particular spirit for a particular person. I cannot control when they give me messages. Also, I cannot channel, get predictions, or find lost objects.

My wife can sometimes hear, feel, smell and more rarely see entities. Susan can get messages from dreams occasionally. She has been known to Channel, but she cannot control when it happens. She is unable to get predictions, messages from other means or find lost objects. She is unable to control the when and how of her abilities.

There are also a lot of charlatans that claim abilities that they do not have. They believe that they can get away with this, because, "who is going to know?" Well the people who really do have the abilities will know. So always check around, there will be rumors about the charlatans. And if there is no one around to ask, trust your instinct. Most psychics are not charlatans. Some psychics are good at what they do and some psychics are exceptional.

An example of a good clairvoyant was a woman who heard about me from the people who owned the metaphysical shop in California several years after that shoot. She called me and asked me to photograph her while she conducted a channeling session. This woman's channeling ability was so strong that she was sometimes able to lend the spirits enough energy so that they could show themselves to people on this side who generally were unable to see paranormal activity. In these three photographs you can see various examples of entities. The photographs were taken within a five minute span. There were pauses between the photographs because the entity was also giving me messages.

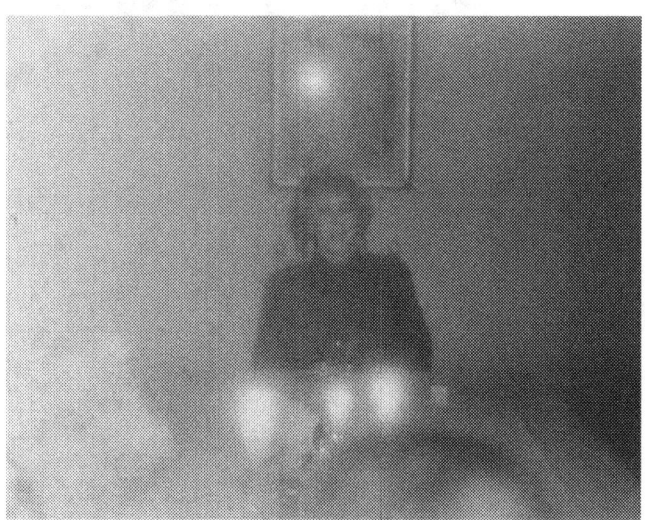

The energy bar on the left and only one ball of energy remains.

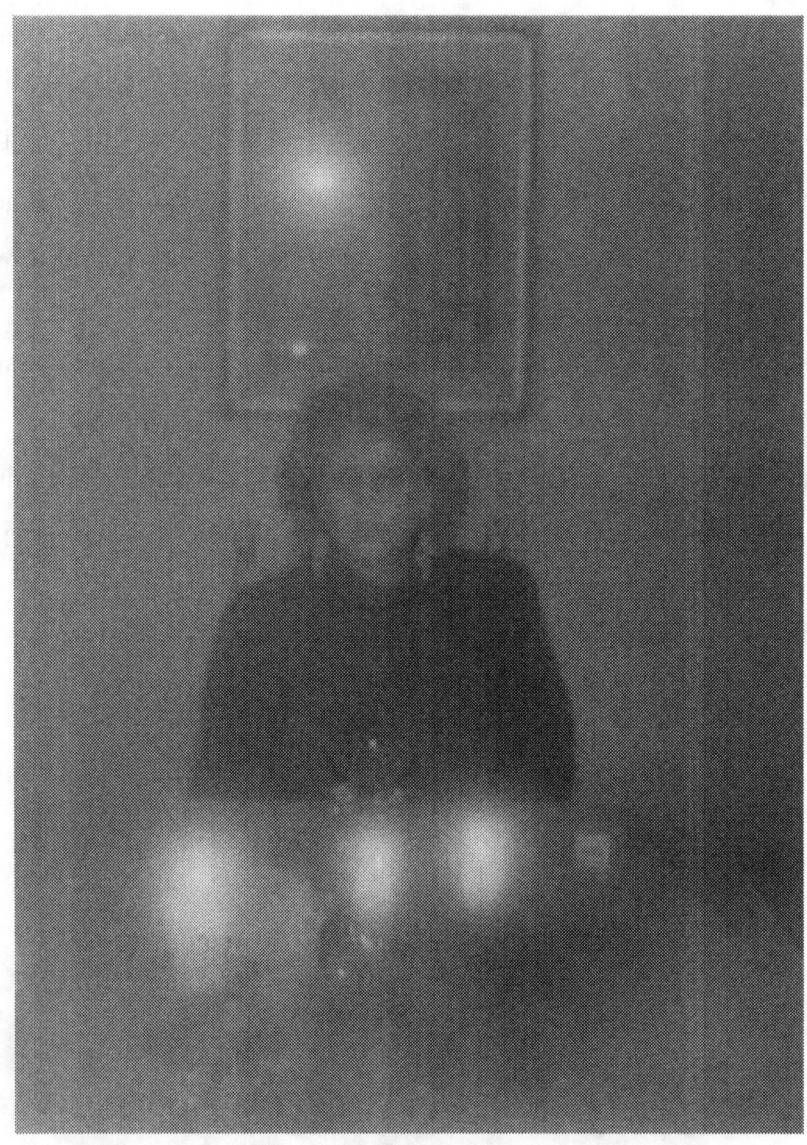

Notice the two balls of energy floating over her head and the overall level of energy in the air that gives a soft focus to the whole image.

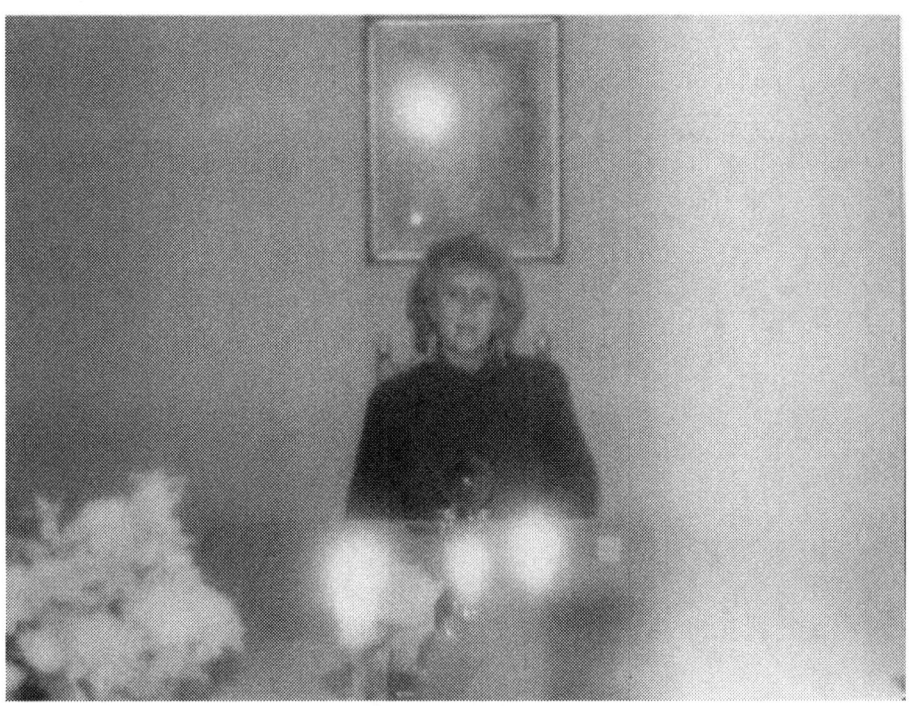

Here you have two balls and a bar of energy with a figure forming at the bottom of the bar next to the man's head. Notice how large the top ball of energy is in this photograph. The top ball is not from a camera flash since no flash was used.

So Called Myths

There are many myths in the world today. Some are indicative of people's imaginations. However, some are based in reality. Such myths as gnomes, fairies and UFOs are true. How do I know? Because, I have pictures or I have just seen them throughout the years. At this time, I do not have any fairy pictures. They are elusive and not prone to allow themselves to be photographed. However, I do have two friends that have some fairies living in their backyards. I have hopes of getting an image of one someday.

Early in the year of 1994, we were living in Colorado Springs, Colorado. Around dinner time, a neighbor knocked on our door and told me, "Hey, you have got to check this out." I ran outside with him and looked around. I saw some strange things in the sky. I ran back into the house and grabbed one of my cameras. This one turned out to be loaded with regular film.

I got six shots of an aircraft that was behaving strangely. It would hover for long periods of time and then suddenly shoot across the sky and then hover again. It zigzagged back and forth for about 20 minutes, and then it just disappeared. The next day, the papers were full of the UFO sightings across the city.

These images presented below and on the next three pages are in the order that I took them.

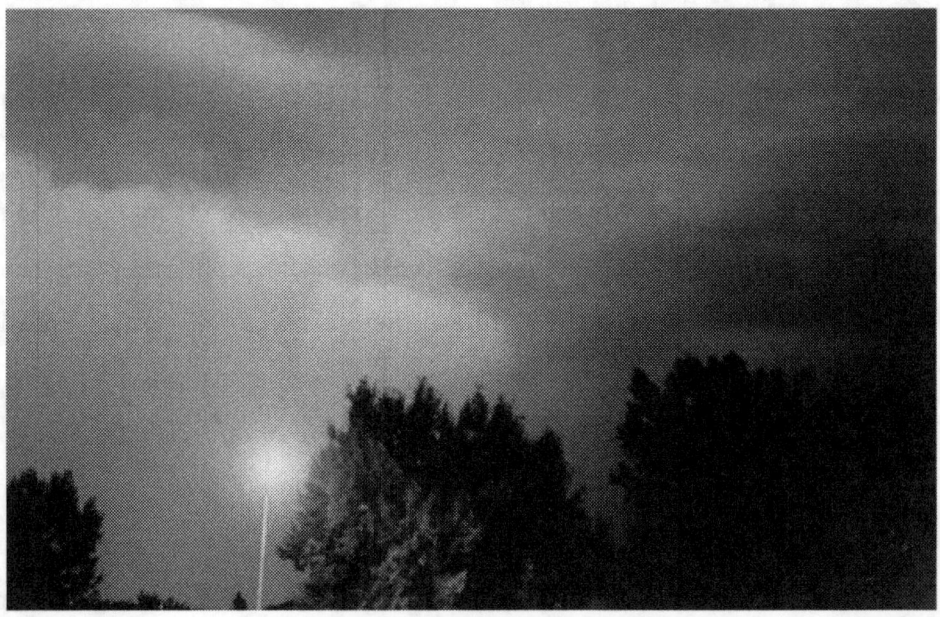

The UFO I located in the upper right corner.

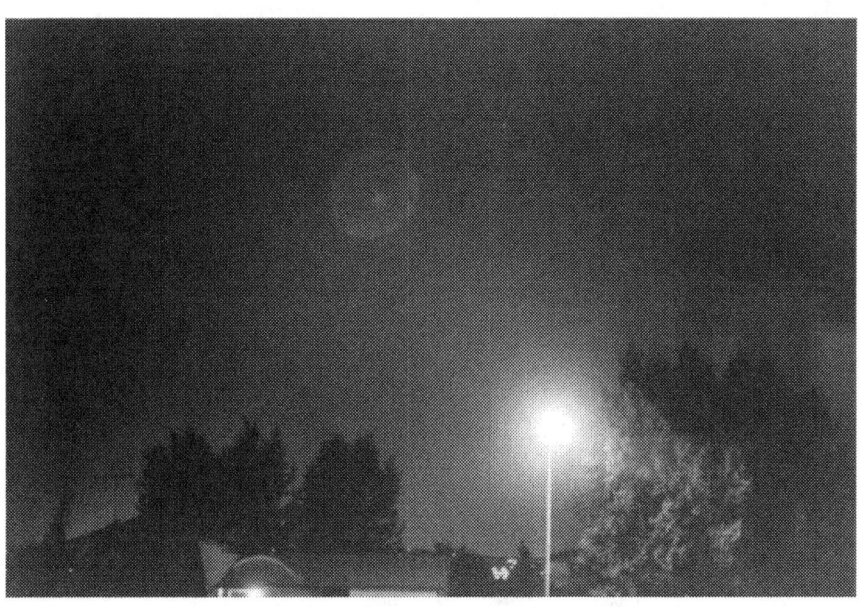

Above the UFO is located in the upper middle of the photograph.

Below the UFO is located in upper left quadrant of this shot.

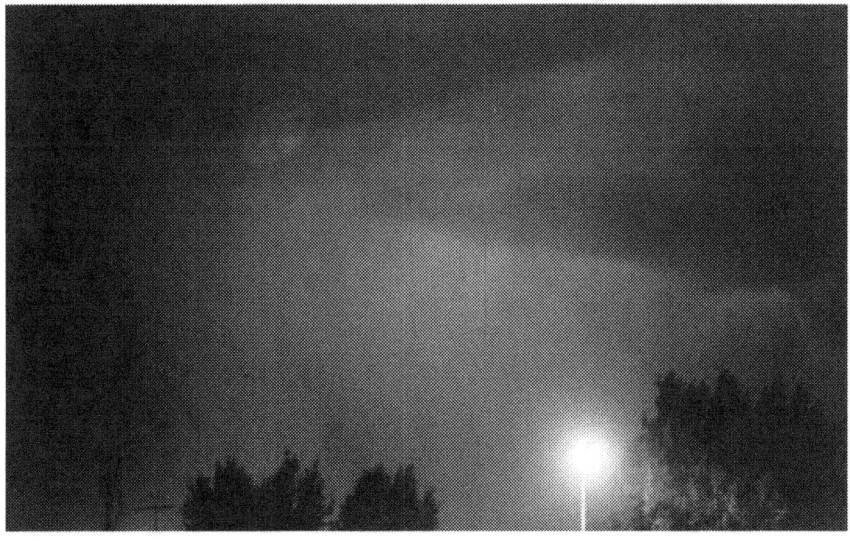

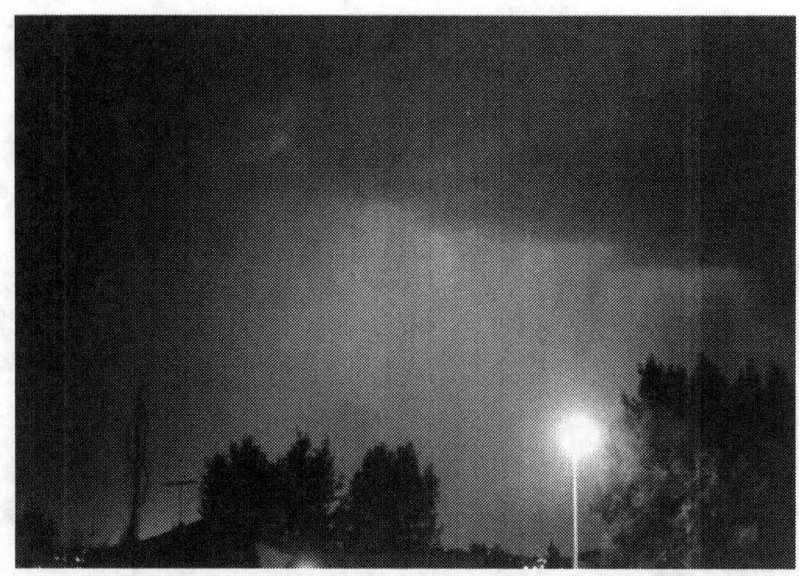

Above the UFO is hovering while the clouds moved.

Below the UFO is located in the space behind the two trees on the right.

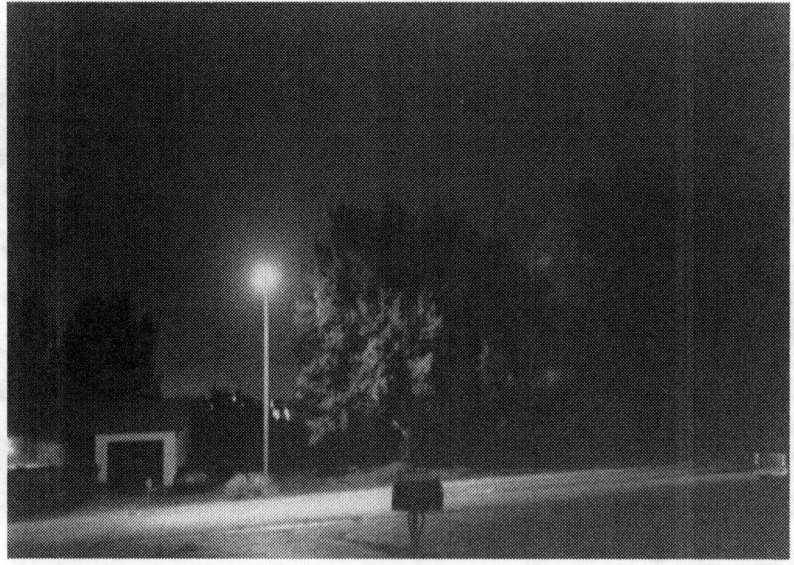

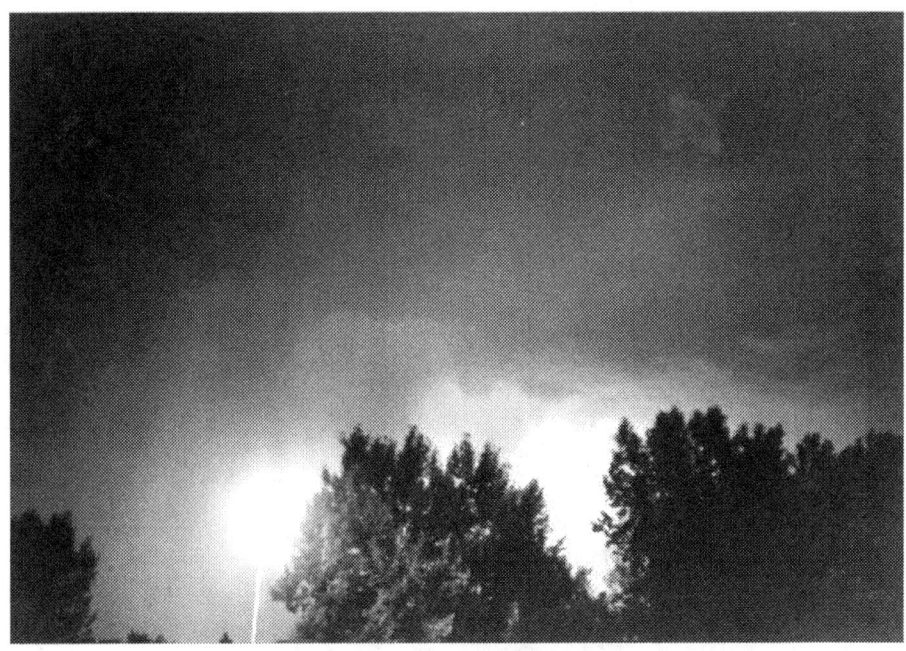

Above the UFO is leaving in the upper right corner just before it disappeared.

Another of the so called myths that I do have on film was taken during a demonstration of an energy device in Aztec, New Mexico in 1997. Another full blooded Cherokee medicine man, who does not wish to be identified, was present during this shoot. He told me that there was a presence and that I should get a shot of it. I also felt the presence, but I could not locate him during the actual shoot. When the photographs were developed, I found him

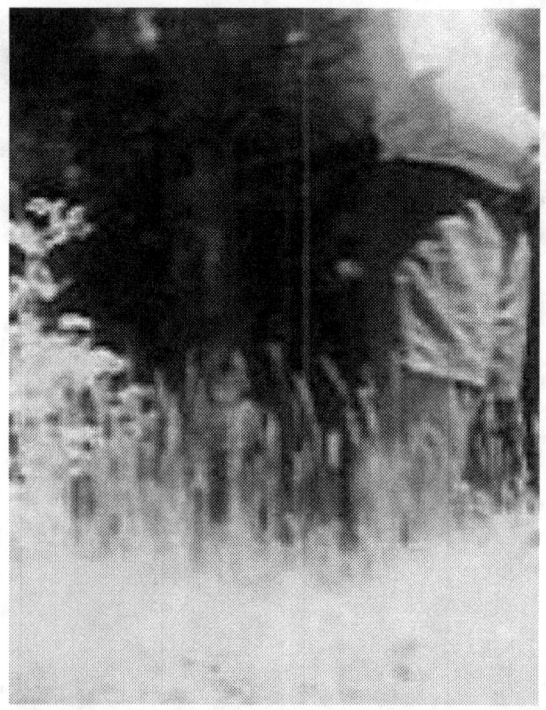

standing behind the man's legs, with the shorts on, and a tall weed. He was standing back under the trees. It was a gnome! This is the image known as the "Aztec Gnome" as seen on page 103. This detail of the "Aztec Gnome" to the left helps locate the gnome. It is located near the center of this frame between the man's knees and the tall weed on the left of the photograph.

This shoot was done on the property of the person who dealt with the energy devices. Since he was scared of the gnome and reluctant to be associated with it, I cannot disclose his name or the exact location.

I have placed the photographs in the order that I took them. In the first image the man that was standing left of the energy device walked away. Immediately, the other man in shorts walked up. This is when the gnome showed up to see what was going on. Within a couple of minutes the first man walked back over next to the man with the shorts. You can still see part of the gnome peeking out between those two men's legs on page 104.

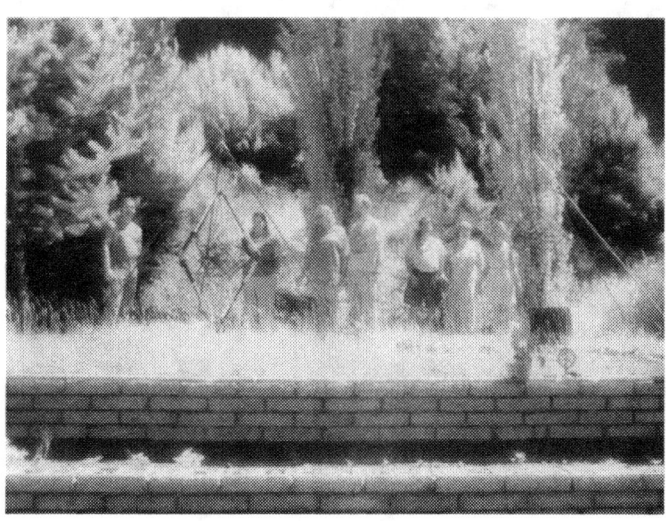

The man standing left of the energy device walks away.

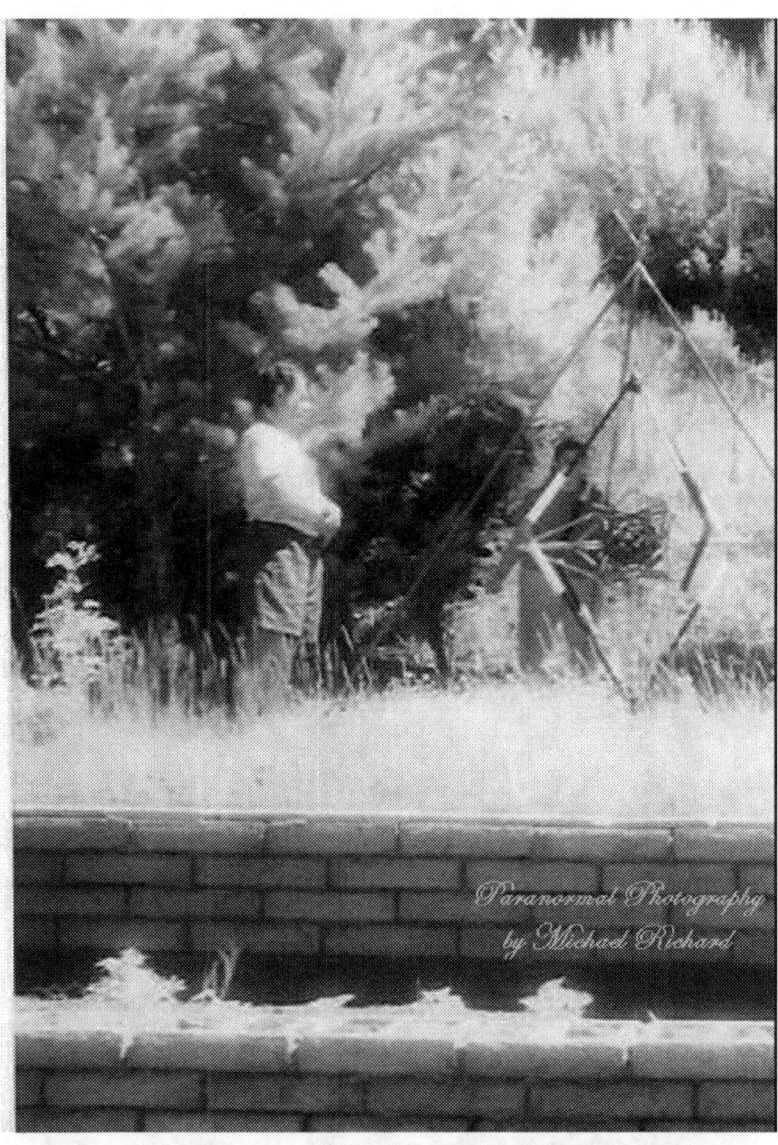

Another man walks up and stands by the energy device and shows the gnome
standing behind him in this photograph known as "Aztec Gnome."

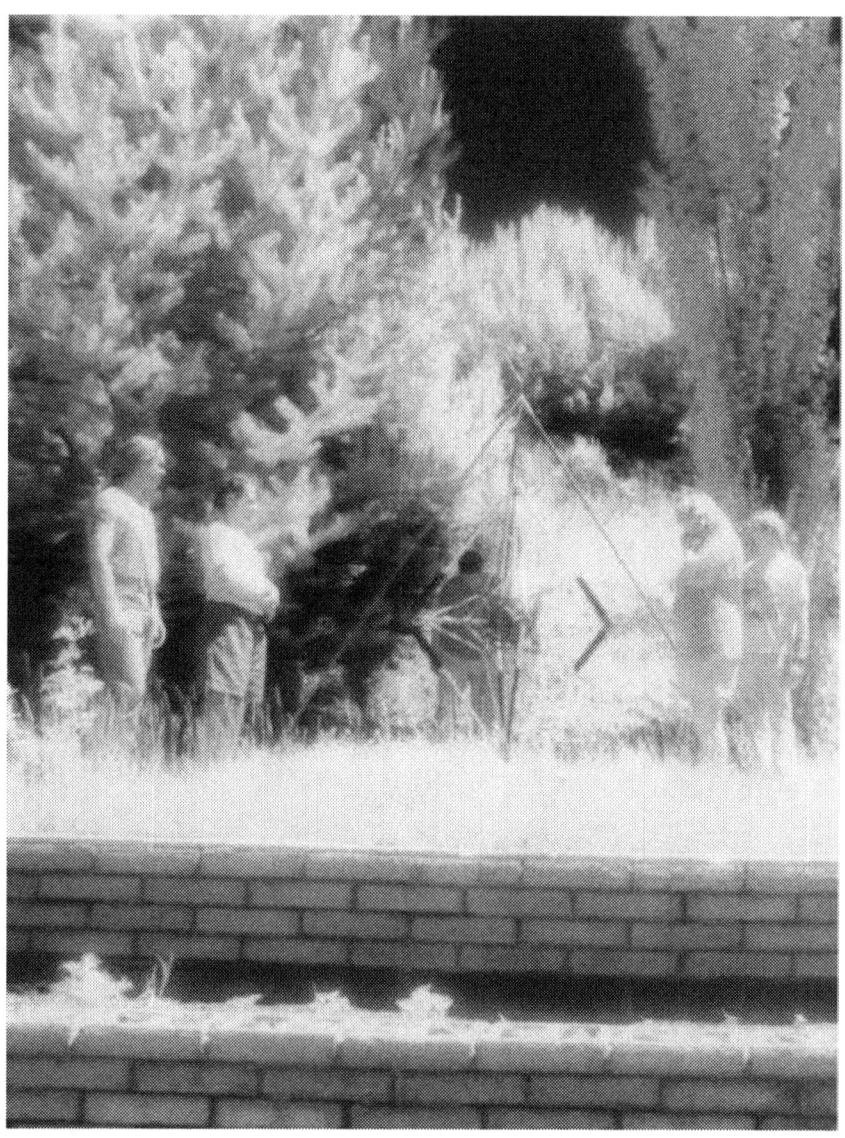

*This frame shows that the first man has come back into the frame
and the gnome looking out from between the two men.*

Epilogue

We all seek the world of the paranormal. It's amazing how many people go through life looking for signs from the other side, when in actuality, it's there everyday. All we have to do is pay attention to our surroundings.

Everyday there is a new opportunity open to everyone in both this world and the paranormal world. I come across so many paranormal activities because I pay attention to all that surrounds me. Also, the spirits will use the opportunities they find, including using my work to communicate to those on this side.

Reading this book may be an opening experience for you or perhaps for a friend. Anytime you're investigating a haunted place show respect for the living as well as the spirits - Don't make a lot of noise - Don't bring in your fancy equipment. You need to learn to trust your instincts.   Doing this will help you have a more memorable time.

May all your dreams come true!

www.ingramcontent.com/pod-product-compliance
Lightning Source LLC
Chambersburg PA
CBHW072035190526
45165CB00017B/940